CANOEING IN ONTARIO

IAN SCOTT
MAVIS KERR

illustrations by Elaine Macpherson

Greey de Pencier Publications 1975 Toronto
59 Front Street East, Toronto

Printed in Canada
ISBN 0-919872-12-3

Art direction: Ron Butler and Wendy Pease

First Printing: March 1975
Second Printing: June 1975

We, the authors, would particularly like to thank John McRuer, the central figure of our canoe-tripping organization, Algonquin Waterways Wilderness Trips. As canoe trip leaders with Algonquin Waterways, we have learned much of the information in this book from John.

The assistance of the following is also gratefully acknowledged: Ministry of Natural Resources District Offices and District Conservation Authorities — for their help in compiling the "Where To Canoe" listings; Craig Macdonald, Parks Planning Branch, Ministry of Natural Resources — for his help in proof-reading the maps.

Contents

History

Leaving the dock in a canoe with a picnic lunch is an ideal way to escape from city crowds and pressures. More and more, people are turning to canoeing as an economical way of enjoying the summer months. Now, over half the recreational enquiries received by the Ministry of Natural Resources of the Ontario government concern canoeing. In Algonquin Park alone, the number of canoeists has more than doubled since 1969. Many Canadians see the canoe as the ideal vehicle to wilderness, wildlife, and solitude.

But canoeing has not always been a recreational activity. Long before the white man set foot in what is now Ontario, Algonquin Indians relied on birch bark canoes, sewn together with spruce roots and sealed with spruce gum, to help them stalk game and maintain their nomadic lifestyle. Their canoes could be carried by one man, and could

easily be repaired in the bush. In their canoes, Indians paddled gracefully along Ontario's waterways, slipping quietly from lake to stream. When Samuel de Champlain first saw the Indians paddling their canoes in 1603, he expressed amazement at their speed and style. In the 17th century, fashions in Europe demanded that the best hats be made of beaver, so the Hudson's Bay Company and the North-West Company searched Canada for new sources of this fur. To carry barter goods to the Indian trappers and furs back to the seaports, the fur trading companies extended the Indian canoe to 36 feet and named it the *canoe de maitre,* or master canoe. These canoes were paddled by voyageurs, romantic figures in Canada's past. Although the voyageurs appeared to have a carefree life, they worked gruelling 16-18 hour days.

In this century, canoeing appeared in a new form. Summer camps flourished in central Ontario for the children of Ontario's urban families. At these camps, canoes made of traditional cedar and canvas were used to take campers into Ontario's wilderness. Canoeing and summer camps became synonymous. Then, with easier access to Ontario's north, canoeing became a recreational activity for the city dweller wishing to escape urban pressures. More leisure time and a new interest in self-propelled means of transportation makes canoeing for Ontario residents and visitors alike, an inexpensive and popular activity for all ages.

Types of canoeing

Canoeing is one of those activities that can be enjoyed at many different levels. As long as you're in a long narrow boat that can be propelled by paddles and is light enough to carry, you're canoeing. There are four broad types of canoeing to choose from: canoe touring, kayaking, competitive canoeing and whitewater canoeing.

Canoe Touring

Canoe touring, or recreational canoeing is what this book is all about and it includes everything from spending an afternoon on a pond in a rented canoe to taking a lengthy wilderness trip. A day's outing in a canoe can be safely tackled by anyone with basic paddling skills, while a canoe camping trip requires more planning and a knowledge of wilderness camping skills. Most leisure canoeists use 14 to 17 foot open canoes, travelling two or three to a boat. Under their own power, they can explore outdoor places that power boats can never reach.

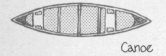

Canoe

Kayaking

Kayakers can enjoy most of the pleasures of canoe touring. Their boats, with covered decks and narrow beams, are fast and are capable of withstanding much rougher water than regular canoes. The disadvantages of kayaks for tripping, however, are that they lack storage space and are awkward to portage.

Kayak

Competitive Canoeing

This sport pits canoeists against the clock and each other. For the young and hardy with a competitive spirit, it's a good sport and the best way to get involved is to join a club (see page 78).

Racing Canoe

Whitewater Canoeing

Whitewater canoeing embraces running and rerunning the same set of rapids all day, or running rapids encountered on a wilderness canoe trip. Naturally, this can be dangerous, but there are well-developed techniques used in whitewater canoeing, and they are taught by professionals (see page 79). Some experienced canoeists combine whitewater canoeing and racing - this is as exciting as it sounds.

Choosing equipment

Canoeing is a sport with a rich heritage, and over the years many different styles of canoes have developed. On the one hand we have the purists who sneer at any canoe not made of the traditional cedar strip while others, the more practical-minded, say that the most important feature of a canoe is its lightness.

The basic design of canoes has not changed since the days when they were used exclusively by Indians, but new synthetic materials permit much more strength than the traditional wood and birch-bark.The important thing is to understand the options available before determining what's best for you. Some will prefer a large canoe made of a tough material like aluminum that is designed to withstand extended wilderness trips, while others will want a short light canoe that children can handle easily.

When shopping for your canoe and related equipment, the first rule is to find a reliable store that has a canoeist on staff. Ask this salesperson some questions to which you already know the answers, and if he seems knowledgeable, listen to his advice. That person's help, along with what you learn here, should enable you to make the right purchase.

Take time to look around. Talk to friends who have some canoeing experience. Ask the opinion of outfitters who own and maintain a number of canoes, or find a manufacturer who will allow you to try out some canoes on a nearby body of water.

Most retail outlets for canoes can be found in the *Yellow Pages* under "Boat Dealers"; suppliers of other equipment are listed under "Camping Equipment".

As a rule, you get what you pay for. If your jerrybuilt canoe springs a leak, you could be miles from anywhere, and an inexpensive paddle that's easily broken could mean a difficult trip home. Remember that your equipment is an investment that will, with care, last a lifetime.

For some people renting may be the solution. Some retailers will outfit you, and you can also rent equipment at many of the conservation areas and parks listed in this book. The *Ontario Canada Camping Book* (see tear-out page) gives a complete listing of Ontario outfitters. Canoe rentals usually run about $7 a day.

Canoes

Your canoe is the most expensive piece of equipment you'll need and can present the new canoeist with buying problems. There are all sorts of options and very few guidelines. At the present time, there aren't even any federal laws governing canoe safety. The most important features to look for are mentioned below but if you're at all in doubt about what canoe to buy contact Allied Boating Canada at 4800 Dundas St. W., Toronto, 416-236-2497. This group certifies canoes that it considers seaworthy.

Material

Wood - Wood is the traditional material for canoes and for some canoeists a cedar strip canoe has a "feel" that no others come close to. Cedar strip planks and ribs are used to produce the body. A canvas exterior waterproofs the canoe. Although aesthetically pleasing, cedar strip canoes absorb water, thereby gaining weight during their lives. They are somewhat fragile and require more maintenance than other canoes. Expect to pay from $400 up.

Fibreglass - Fibreglass canoes have the largest variation in price and there is a wide range of manufacturing craftsmanship. There are two common methods of construction: the hand lay up method and the chopped glass process. Choose the hand lay up method. Generally you can identify this construction type because the interior fibreglass cloth is more apparent - but still it is wise to ask about the canoe you're looking at.

When manufacturers use the chopped glass process, they blow fine strands of fibreglass into a canoe mold. This results in a much more irregular distribution of fibreglass than the hand lay up method so the finished product is not as resilient.

There are also two different kinds of fibreglass resins used - polyester and epoxy. Epoxy cures (or hardens) more slowly than polyester and is therefore less brittle - but only an expert can really tell the difference, so again, ask.

An epoxy canoe made by the hand lay up method combines some of the beauty of the cedar strip canoe with most of the strength of aluminum. Expect to pay from $350 up.

Aluminum - Pound for pound, aluminum is the strongest material of all. Whitewater canoeists almost exclusively choose aluminum for

Canoes
Continued

open canoes. Again, manufacturing and craftsmanship are important. Thin aluminum (less than 40/1000 inch) will dent easily so be sure to get something more substantial. Also check that the canoe is of stretch form, not cut form construction. The former means that the two sheets of aluminum are stretched in a mold and then welded into one piece. This guarantees a faster canoe because of cleaner lines and bilateral symmetry. A stretch form canoe also has fewer joints and therefore is lighter and has less chance of leaking. Also be sure that there are no unfinished edges under the gunwales, decks and seats. Rough edges catch skin and clothing. The riveting on the seams should be close together.

Because an aluminum canoe reflects light, you may want to paint its decks to reduce glare. One negative aspect of aluminum is that some people complain about the noise - they liken it to "paddling a garbage can". The best aluminum canoes are made in the U.S., so prices are higher here in Canada. Expect to pay at least $375.

Design
Canoes don't all have the same shape. Differences in design will

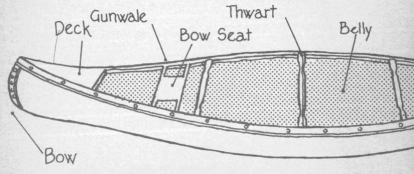

affect speed, manoeuverability, and safety in rough water. Here are some pointers.

• A good canoe should have the capacity to carry at least 650 pounds, i.e. three adults with some gear, and still maintain at least six inches of freeboard. If you are considering longer trips, or running rapids, you will want a canoe with a still larger capacity.

• Your canoe should be at least 15 feet long. Smaller canoes with more than two adults in them, can be dangerous. And surprisingly, larger canoes are easier to paddle because they ride higher in the water with the same load.

• The average beam (distance at widest point) is about 34 inches on a 16-foot canoe. A novice might consider a canoe with an even wider beam. This will give more stability and a larger loading capacity. However, the wider the canoe the more sluggish its performance. The broad beam meets greater resistance as it moves through the water.

• A narrow canoe in the hands of the inexperienced canoeist tends to roll like a log. Beginners should look for a flat-bottomed canoe, again, for reasons of stability.

• On some canoes you will see a

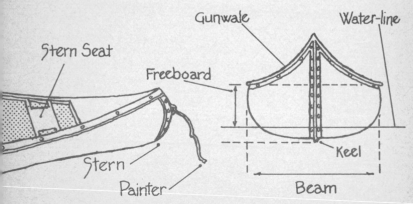

Canoes

Continued

high bow and stern. These features are not necessary. Contrary to what you might think, a bow that flares upwards doesn't prevent water from splashing into the canoe in rough weather. In fact a high bow and stern can cause you to be buffeted about in a cross-wind.

• Indians had thwarts in their canoes rather than seats. This forced them to sit or kneel on the bottom of their canoes. Seats are provided nowadays, but sometimes they are improperly placed. They should be positioned below the gunwales (pronounced gunnels) but high enough so that you can comfortably tuck your feet back under them.

• Your canoe should have a depth of at least a foot at the centre thwart. A shallower canoe cannot safely hold much weight.

• A keel keeps a canoe moving in a straight line, but also reduces manoeuverability. So look for a canoe with one small keel in the centre. It will aid control in windy weather.

In sum, a novice would do best with a canoe at least 15 feet long with at least a 34 inch beam and a small keel. The belly should be fairly flat.

Weight

Canoes vary in weight between 40 and 95 lbs., depending on size and material. Generally, cedar strip canoes are heavier than aluminum or fibreglass canoes of the same size. A 16-foot canoe should not weigh more than 65 lbs. No one wants a heavy canoe on a portage. However, some canoes sacrifice strength for ultra-lightness. New materials have allowed the manufacture of very light canoes, but be cautious. Some just won't stand up to any kind of extended use.

Flotation

Fibreglass and aluminum canoes are not naturally buoyant. They need positive flotation, which means some kind of buoyant material. such as styrofoam. Avoid air chamber flotation as these chambers are easily filled with water. Positive flotation is usually placed under the bow and stern decks. Some canoes have strips of positive flotation tacked below the gunwales on the outside of the canoe. These canoes are certainly more stable, but are also more awkward to paddle.

Other basic equipment

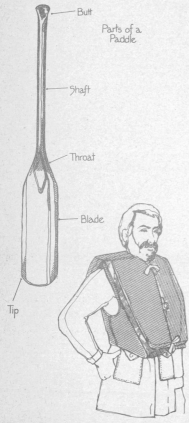

Butt

Parts of a Paddle

Shaft

Throat

Blade

Tip

A good lifejacket should hold your head above water

Paddles

As a rule of thumb, your paddle should reach from the ground to your nose when you are standing straight. But different body proportions mean that this rule is only approximate. It's not really important for beginners to know about blade shape but you should know that the width of a good paddle blade should not exceed seven inches. With wider paddles you will tire quickly. Racers use wider blades to paddle quickly, but they are also well-trained before the season.

A laminated softwood paddle is the best combination of strength and lightness. Expect to pay between $10 and $14.

Lifejackets

Make it a personal rule to always carry Department of Transport approved lifejackets in your canoe. These lifejackets don't have to be worn all the time, but should be available for rough weather or fast water. Non-swimmers, of course, should always wear lifejackets. The most expensive are vests designed for sailing and they can be worn comfortably all the time. Prices vary between $9 and $30.

Getting launched

Carrying and Launching

To carry a canoe a short distance, such as from the car to the water's edge, two canoeists can grasp the gunwales on either side of the centre thwart. Lifting should be done with the back and legs, not just with the arms. Once you get to the water, your canoe is best launched perpendicular to the shore. This is easy. Simply lower the bow of the canoe and slide your hands up the gunwales to the stern so the canoe slides into the water. If you aren't departing immediately, tie the canoe securely!

Weight Distribution

Place the packs in the belly of your canoe near the centre thwart and below the gunwales. This keeps the canoe well trimmed and its weight low. Ideally the stern of your loaded canoe should be slightly heavier than the bow. This gives the sternsperson more effective control. Windy weather changes this situation because the heaviest end will always try to point into the wind. If you are paddling into the wind, rearrange your load so that the bow is heavier than the stern.

Lift from the centre for a short carry

Launch the bow first

Entering and Positioning

Before climbing into your canoe, make sure that it is fully afloat. If it's partly on land, it's not only very unstable, but there is also the possibility of forcing a rock up through its belly when you step in. For the same reason, load your gear with your canoe fully afloat. Load packs first so that your crew can properly stabilize the canoe from shore. If you're entering from a dock, draw the canoe parallel to the dock. With the bowperson steadying the canoe from the dock, the sternsperson steps into the middle of the canoe just in front of the stern seat. He keeps his weight low. After

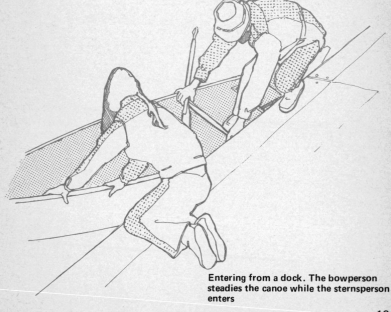

Entering from a dock. The bowperson steadies the canoe while the sternsperson enters

Getting launched

Continued

the sternsperson is kneeling in the
canoe, he holds onto the dock and
balances the canoe while the bowperson enters in a similar fashion.
Often it's necessary to enter a
canoe from shore. Making sure the
canoe is fully afloat, the sternsperson stands on shore and steadies
the canoe while the bowperson
places his paddle across the gunwales and steps into the canoe. It's
easy to tip a canoe at this point, so
make sure that your first step is to
the centre of the canoe (above the
centre keel). You can now walk the
length of the canoe, keeping your
weight low and using the paddle to
steady yourself. When the bowperson is kneeling, the sternsperson
climbs in.

To get out, reverse the procedure.

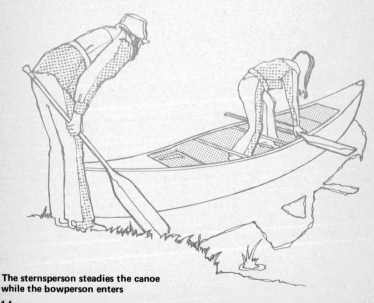

**The sternsperson steadies the canoe
while the bowperson enters**

Paddling Position

Kneeling lowers your weight, making the canoe more stable, and it keeps your knees out of the way of your strokes. This low centre of gravity becomes very important in rough weather and fast water. (For fun, sometime, try lying in the bottom of your canoe and then try to tip it. It's reassuring to know that it's virtually impossible to do.)

For calm, flat water canoeing, you will probably find it more comfortable to switch between the sitting and kneeling positions. This gives your legs a rest. When sitting, cross your ankles so that your knees are below the gunwales.

If you can have a face to face conversation with your canoeing partner, there's something the matter. Both canoeists should be facing *toward* the bow. You should also be paddling on opposite sides of the boat holding the paddle as in the diagram below. The hand at the top of the paddle is referred to as the butt hand, and the one near the blade is the throat hand.

Butt Hand

Throat Hand

Proper paddling position

Paddling technique

Most beginners can make a canoe move, even if a little awkwardly. However, when you want to travel straight from one place to another and your canoe insists on zig-zag-ging, it's useful to know some of the common strokes. If executed properly, these strokes will give you control and make canoeing a more relaxed sport for you.

Power Stroke

A good power stroke makes the difference between feeling sluggish by noon, or still full of zip at the end of the day. It has a natural rhythm and you will catch on eas-ily. Study the diagrams here care-fully before setting out.

Start the stroke with the paddle a comfortable distance in front of you without leaning forward (as in diagram 1). The paddle should be

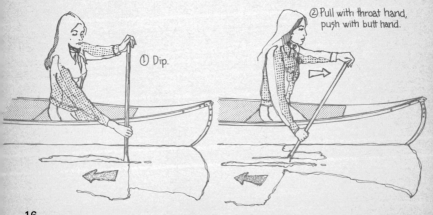

① Dip.

② Pull with throat hand, push with butt hand.

vertical and as close to the canoe as possible with the blade at least three-quarters submerged. Pull with your throat arm and push with your butt arm (as in diagram 2). Lean into the stroke with your body instead of doing all the work with your arms. When your throat hand is beside your hip, lift the paddle out of the water by lowering your butt hand, (as in diagram 3). Keeping your paddle as horizontal as possible and the paddle tip just above the water (as in diagram 4), bring the paddle back to the starting position and take your next stroke. Some of the common problems are leaning too far forward and failing to extend the arms at the beginning of the stroke.

The power stroke is used by all paddlers other than the sternsperson, who uses a variation of the power stroke called the J-stroke.

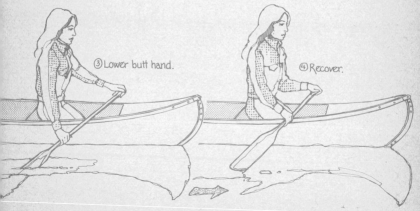

③ Lower butt hand.

④ Recover.

Paddling technique
Continued

J-Stroke

When you first start to canoe, it will seem that your canoe has a mind of its own. This is because, if paddlers are of equal strength, the sternsperson will overpower the bowperson because of the stern's favourable leverage - i.e. the canoe will constantly veer right if the sternsperson is paddling on the left. There are many inefficient methods of keeping a canoe on a straight course. The sternsperson can use the paddle as a rudder, or both paddlers can continually change sides. The Indians solved this problem by inventing the J-stroke. The sternsperson simply carves the letter J in the water with his paddle while the bowperson continues the basic power stroke. The J-stroke may seem difficult at first but, with practice, it's easy. Experiment with the J-stroke on both sides of the canoe.

Starting in the regular power position, (see *Power Stroke*), bring the paddle back to your hip, as in diagram 3. When your throat hand is beside your hip, turn the submerged blade 90 degrees by twisting

① Dip.   ② Power Stroke.

your butt wrist so that your thumb is pointing down as in diagram 3. The paddle is now parallel to your canoe like a rudder, with the submerged blade offering the least possible resistance to the water. Now pull the butt of the paddle across your body, forcing the blade away from the canoe. This part of the stroke, called the pry, causes the bow to swing toward the side on which the sternsperson is paddling.

Some paddlers rest their paddle shaft against the gunwale, using the gunwale as a fulcrum. How much you pry depends on how much you want to swing the bow. To recover from the pry, twist your wrists up, so that the blade can easily slip out of the water as in diagram 4. This stroke should be a rhythmic one.

With the sternsperson performing a J-stroke and the bowperson the power stroke, canoeists paddling in unison and on opposite sides, should be able to keep a straight course. If you are a sternsperson and are having difficulty keeping pace with the bowperson, shorten the power part of your stroke or simply ask him to slow down.

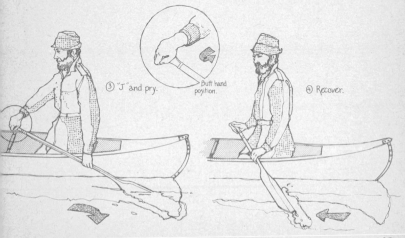

③ "J" and pry. Butt hand position.

④ Recover.

Paddling technique
Continued

Stopping

Sooner or later you will need to stop your canoe quickly. Whether you are the bow or sternsperson, if you want a fast stop, shout, "Hold water!" Both you and your partner should then plunge the blades of your paddles into the water close to your sides so the blades offer the most resistance to the water. Angle your paddles so that your butt hand is just in front of your butt shoulder as in the diagram, and hold on tight. You're fighting momentum, but if both of you angle your paddle correctly, the canoe should stop without turning to either one side or the other.

Stopping your canoe

Sweep Stroke

To turn your canoe, you use sweep strokes. They are most often used when the canoe is stationary or when you are leaving a dock. There are front sweeps and back sweeps for both bow and stern. When the bow and sternsperson perform opposite sweeps on opposite sides of the canoe, they can spin the canoe without it moving forward or backwards. The sweep stroke is slightly different, depending on whether you're in the bow or stern.

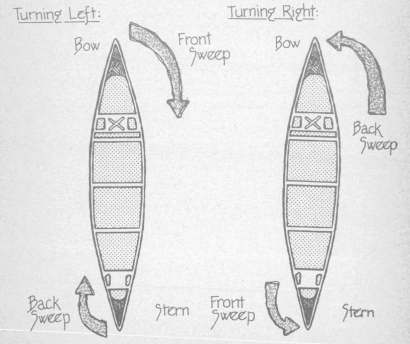

Turning Left:

Bow Front Sweep

Back Sweep Stern

Turning Right:

Bow Back Sweep

Front Sweep Stern

Paddling technique
Continued

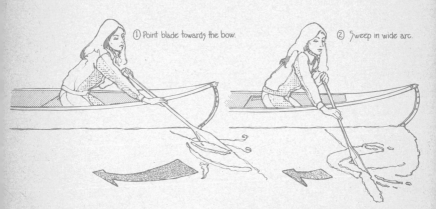

① Point blade towards the bow.

② Sweep in wide arc.

Turning to the Left
If you're in the bow, a front sweep stroke on the right side directs the canoe to your left.

With your throat hand about a foot up the shaft from the blade, lean forward, and point the blade toward the bow tip of the canoe as in diagram 1. Lower the paddle blade to just below the surface of the water, keeping the blade as horizontal as possible. Sweep the paddle in a wide quarter circle until it is opposite your hip as in diagram 3. Lift the blade out of the water and return to the starting position as in diagram 4.

If you're in the stern, you can help

A. Back sweep in stern

B. Back sweep in bow

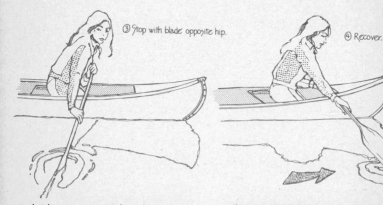

③ Stop with blade opposite hip.

④ Recover.

the bowperson swing the canoe with a back sweep on the left side as in diagram A. As in the front sweep, move your throat hand about a foot up the shaft. Reverse your throat hand grip. This makes it easier to push the paddle forward. Start the stroke from the stern tip of the canoe and push the submerged paddle in a wide quarter circle towards the bow. Lift it out when it reaches your hips.

Turning to the Right

In the bow, use a back sweep stroke on your right side as in diagram B. Move your throat hand up the shaft, reverse your hand grip, and push the paddle in a wide quarter circle from your hips to the bow tip of the canoe. The sternsperson can assist with a front sweep on his left side as in diagram C. Start your stroke from your hips and draw the paddle in a wide arc to the stern tip of the canoe.

If both sets of strokes are done slowly in unison and on opposite sides, the canoe will turn quickly and smoothly.

C. Front sweep in stern

Paddling technique
Continued

Putting It all Together

With the skills illustrated on the previous pages, two people should be able to paddle in a straight line veering when they want. The sternsperson captains the ship and controls the direction. The diagrams below recap the necessary strokes. With more than two paddlers in a canoe, make sure they choose paddling sides so that their paddles don't bump one another.

Paddling Straight Ahead:

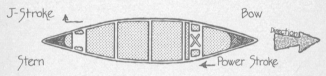

J-Stroke

Bow

Direction

Stern

Power Stroke

Veering Left When Moving:

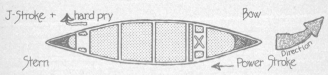

J-Stroke + hard pry

Bow

Direction

Stern

Power Stroke

Veering Right When Moving:

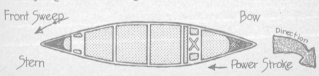

Front Sweep

Bow

Direction

Stern

Power Stroke

Solo Canoeing

It's satisfying to be able to control a canoe proficiently on your own, but it does take a lot of practice. To try solo paddling, kneel at the bow seat of your canoe *facing the stern* so that your weight is closer to the boat's centre thwart. (If you stay in the stern, the bow sticks up in the air and acts as a sail, making your canoe difficult to control.) By using a J-stroke with an extended pry, you can keep your canoe on a straight course without having to change sides. Experienced solo canoeists use a whole range of specialized 'rokes. Until you're an expert, solo a canoe only on a calm day within easy reach of a help.

What if You Tip?

If you keep your weight low in the canoe you shouldn't tip. Nevertheless it can happen to the best of us. In fact, it's a good idea to practise tipping intentionally. The first rule is to put on your lifejacket or make sure it's handy.

If you tip close to shore, hold onto your canoe and swim it to a place where you can take it out of the water. Worry about your gear only when you're safe. With the help of a friend, turn the canoe sideways so that water will drain out of it as you lift it out of the water. If the canoe is completely upside down you'll find when you try to lift it that outside air pressure holds water inside until the entire boat is above the water, greatly increasing its weight. Tilt your canoe to break the seal and it will be much easier to lift. When your canoe is drained, right it and ease it back into the water.

If you are far away from shore when you tip, hold onto your canoe and signal for help. *Never* leave your canoe and try to swim for shore. It's always further than you think. There are methods of emptying a swamped canoe in the middle of a lake, and rescuing a canoe using another canoe. These methods are complicated and not techniques for the beginner. Some of the books recommended on page 78 will give you this information.

Portaging

Portaging a canoe from one body of water to another is not as difficult as it may seem, so don't be discouraged by the idea. If the distance is more than a few yards, it is more efficient for one person to lift the canoe onto his shoulders rather than having two people carrying it upright from the bow and stern. With the canoe on your shoulders, your entire back and shoulders help support the load. Two people can carry a canoe on their shoulders but there are problems - unless both have exactly the same stride they will be continually banging their shoulders against the thwart or seat.

There are a few tricks that make carrying a canoe relatively easy. By lashing the paddles into the boat, you can distribute the weight of the canoe more evenly onto your shoulders and back. Some canoes have yokes for this purpose. Wearing a vest lifejacket eases the burden and acts as padding.

Swinging a canoe onto your shoulders requires more coordination than sheer muscle power if you follow these steps: Standing adjacent to the bow seat as in diagram 1, lift the bow onto your knees as in diagram 2. Then, grasp the gunwale beside the bow seat, and with your

Paddles lashed into the canoe with rope.

① Start near bow seat.

Bow

② Lift onto knees.

hand nearest the bow, reach across and grasp the gunwale on the far side as in 3. You are now facing the stern, which is still resting on the ground. Now comes the tricky part - and you can't stop in the middle of this step. By rocking the canoe with your knees and using your arms, swing the bow of the boat above your head as in 4. Simultaneously, your body will twist so that you will end up facing the bow. Step back until you can feel the thwart above your shoulders. Slowly lower the bow of the canoe until the stern lifts off the ground as in 5. Shift the canoe until the bow and stern are equally balanced. You are up and away. Step carefully with your new load.

To get the canoe down off your shoulders, first raise the bow so that the stern touches the ground. By lifting the canoe at the bow seat, raise it off your shoulders. Now, duck your head, and in one motion, roll the canoe onto your knees so that it is upright. You are now facing the stern, which has remained on the ground. Slowly lower the rest of the canoe to the ground.

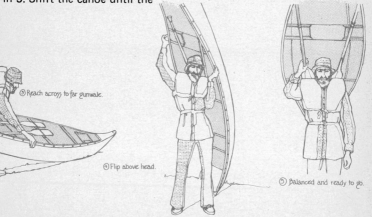

③ Reach across to far gunwale.

④ Flip above head.

⑤ Balanced and ready to go.

Camping

Once you have a canoe, paddles and lifejackets, and a few basic canoeing skills you are ready to tackle any day outing and soon, you will want to venture out for longer periods involving overnight camping. The following section is a guide to assembling the gear necessary to make those camp-outs a comfortable as well as an enjoyable experience.

Seasons, of course, affect your choice of equipment. Warm nights are rare. Be prepared for the worst and you will be happy in any weather or season. Here is what to expect during the canoeing months.

May - Cold nights, more than average rain. Blackflies appear towards the end of the month. Because vegetation is young and tender, it is a good time to gather edible wild foods. Spring run-off swells the rivers and lakes with icy cold water, making more areas accessible. However, tipping can be dangerous.

June - Insect's heaven. The blackflies are out in full force, joined by mosquitoes. In central and northern areas, the deer flies and "no-see-ums" (tiny sand flies) strengthen the bug brigade. As a consolation, the weather is warmer and dryer. It is the best time to see wild flowers in bloom and birds nesting.

July and August - Days are hot and nights warm. Blackflies disappear toward the middle of July and mos-

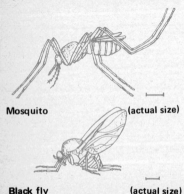

Mosquito   (actual size)

Black fly   (actual size)

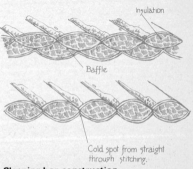

Insulation

Baffle

Cold spot from straight through stitching.

Sleeping bag construction

quitoes linger until the middle of August. Recreational areas are very crowded.

September - In our opinion, the best time of year. The bugs and crowds have all but vanished. Canoeing is one of the best ways to see the autumn leaves. However, nights can be quite cold and many areas that are navigable in mid-summer are now too dry for canoeing.

Sleeping Bags

Sleeping bags keep you warm by effectively holding your body heat within an enclosed area. The best way of insulating your body from the cold is to put a layer of dead air space between you and the weather. Many products, from steel wool to fibreglass, can hold dead air, but only down feathers can hold this dead air and also be compressed into a very small area. A down sleeping bag can be tightly rolled, and will expand to its full loft when needed. Depending on your body metabolism, 1½ pounds of down will keep you warm at 35°F (2°C). For those allergic to down, polyester fill is a good alternative. It is an excellent insulator, although it doesn't have the capacity to be tightly compressed.

Sleeping bags are available in either a rectangular or mummy design. While a mummy is more confining than a rectangular bag, it increases insulating efficiency. Better bags have "baffles" between the inner and outer lining. These baffles mean that the down is distributed evenly, and that there are no cold spots at the stitching. More expensive bags have a flap over the zipper to further minimize heat loss. Carefully consider these design features if you plan to sleep out in May or October. For a good summer bag expect to pay about $40.

A sleeping bag liner keeps the inside of your bag clean. You can make one by folding and sewing a sheet. Wash your liner as you would a regular bedsheet.

Underpadding

It ensures a soft bed on any terrain and keeps you off the cold ground. Padding need only extend from hips to shoulders. Air mattresses take up little room when packed, but have a habit of deflating in the middle of the night. Foam pads weigh less than air mattresses and are better insulators. However, they are bulky and can absorb water. A new padding called Ensolite is wat-

Camping
Continued

erproof and not as bulky as foam padding. However, some campers find it too thin to be comfortable.

Tents

Until the middle of August, biting insects make a fully enclosed tent a necessity. Tents also offer better rain protection than a tarp or an overturned canoe. To be sure that water won't run through your tent, place a plastic sheet slightly larger than the floor itself on the tent floor. This 3 mil plastic is available at most hardware stores. If the plastic sheet runs partly up the sidewalls, no water will run through in the worst downpours.

Your tent material should be water-resistant, not waterproof. If it is waterproof, there will be interior condensation on cold nights because moisture-laden air cannot escape. A tent fly is a useful item. Spread it over your tent as a second covering - it will shed most rainfall. Buy a tent slightly larger than you think you need. You will appreciate the room on those wet days when you want to stay in your tent and read.

A 7' x 7' tent with sidewalls makes efficient use of space and can easily accommodate two adults with gear. Nylon tents are significantly lighter

and less subject to mildew than canvas ones. So look for a tent with a fly, that doesn't weigh more than eight pounds. Prices start around $60.

Other Useful Items

Rope-For the painters of your canoe, buy ten foot lengths of thick (5/8'') manilla rope. Manilla doesn't kink, and thick rope doesn't bite into your hands. As well as painters, always take at least two 50 foot lengths of polypropylene rope. They are indispensible for clotheslines, hanging food packs and many other uses.

Plastic Bags-Wrap everything you take in plastic. This way, your gear will be at least water-resistant, and hopefully waterproof. Well bagged bedding and food will float for a long time if you tip.

Saw and Axe-The collapsible saws on the market are very useful. An axe is more efficient for splitting wood, but potentially more dangerous. Either should be sharp.

Cooking Pots-Most camping stores sell sets of stacking pots. Because they are light weight and have no protruding handles, they are most useful for camp cooking. Detachable handles allow you to take pots

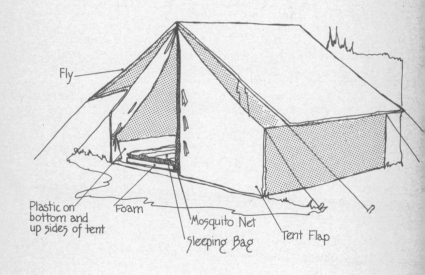

Fly

Plastic on
bottom and
up sides of tent

Foam

Mosquito Net

Sleeping Bag

Tent Flap

Tent prepared for any weather

Camping
Continued

on and off the fire without the handles heating up. Avoid very light weight sets which dent too easily. It is not necessary to clean the outside of your pots. If the exteriors are black, the contents heat faster.

First Aid Kit-A first aid kit can save you a lot of grief. Basic contents are itemized on the *Equipment Check List,* page 34.

Tape-Reinforced book-binding tape has a thousand and one uses. For instance, it can be used to temporarily repair a minor leak in a canoe or hold together a split paddle blade. This is a must for any overnight trip.

Insect Repellent-Buy a brand that has at least 45 per cent active ingredients listed on the label. Only diethyltoluamide and ethyl hexanediol actually keep the bugs away. Avoid repellents that have a high percentage of inert ingredients.

Stove-A small Coleman or Primus stove is handy for outings in highly populated areas where wood is scarce. On longer trips, their bulk and weight are a problem.

Reflector Oven-An oven away from home. This item permits baking of any kind. The reflecting surfaces must be kept as shiny as possible to facilitate high oven temperatures. The reflector oven folds to a ¼ inch thickness when not needed.

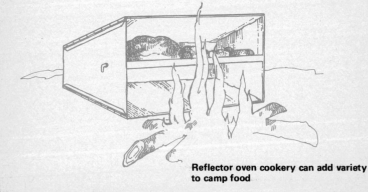

Reflector oven cookery can add variety to camp food

Pack-For day trips, all of your gear should fit into a small back pack. For an overnight trip, a larger pack must be used. Experienced canoeists frown on packs with frames designed for backpacking, because they are difficult to fit into a canoe and don't hold much. Also, when being loaded into a canoe, the frame could puncture the hull. If you are thinking of longer trips with portaging, a canvas tripping bag is best. It should have a double bottom with reinforced stitching at the seams. A good tripping bag of 18 oz. canvas will last you a lifetime. Cost, about $22.

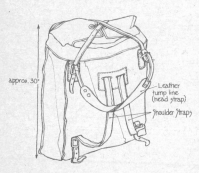

approx. 30"

Leather tump line (head strap)

Shoulder straps

Canoe tripping bag

Lantern and Flashlight-Lanterns are more trouble than they are worth. They are not only fragile and bulky, but require fuel. If you set up camp well before dark, a flashlight will serve your lighting needs. Remember to reverse your batteries when you put your flashlight in your pack. Otherwise flashlights have a nasty habit of turning themselves on when they're jostled inside a pack.

Roof Rack-If you are buying a canoe, you will need a roof rack for your car to move from one place to another. Of course you should be sure to buy one that fits your particular car model.

On the following two pages, there is an Equipment Checklist designed to be photocopied, and on page **41** there is a similar personal clothing checklist. By using these checklists you'll be sure not to forget something essential. Write quantities of each needed item in the left column of each list. Before each outing, round up your equipment and check it off. Check it off again when you pack it into your car. Your needs, of course, will change with the length of your trip and the number of people in your party.

Equipment checklist

Number Needed	Item	Check	Packed
Maps			
_____	Map Case	_____	_____
_____	Maps	_____	_____
_____	Magnetic compass	_____	_____
First Aid Kit			
_____	Triangular Bandages	_____	_____
_____	Sterile Dressings	_____	_____
_____	Adhesive Tape	_____	_____
_____	Needle	_____	_____
_____	Antihistamine	_____	_____
_____	Antibiotic Cream	_____	_____
_____	Sunburn Cream	_____	_____
_____	Aspirin	_____	_____
_____	Salt Pills	_____	_____
_____	Halazone	_____	_____
_____	Calamine Lotion	_____	_____
_____	First aid manual	_____	_____
Cooking and Eating Utensils			
_____	Plastic Mugs	_____	_____
_____	Plastic Bowls	_____	_____
_____	Knives	_____	_____
_____	Forks	_____	_____
_____	Spoons	_____	_____
_____	Stacking Pot Set	_____	_____
_____	Detachable Pot Handle	_____	_____
_____	Frying Pan	_____	_____
_____	Oven Mitts	_____	_____
_____	Serving Spoon	_____	_____
_____	Lifter	_____	_____
_____	Tongs	_____	_____
_____	Can Opener	_____	_____
_____	Cutting Board	_____	_____
_____	Dish Soap	_____	_____
_____	Dish Cloth	_____	_____
_____	Drying Towel	_____	_____
_____	Reflector Oven	_____	_____

Number Needed	Item	Check	Packed
Camping Equipment			
_____	Backpack	_____	_____
_____	Axe	_____	_____
_____	Saw	_____	_____
_____	50' Lengths of Rope	_____	_____
_____	Grill or Bars for Fireplace	_____	_____
_____	Waterproof Matches	_____	_____
_____	Sewing Kit	_____	_____
_____	Heavy Duty Tape	_____	_____
_____	Sharpening Stone	_____	_____
_____	File for Axe	_____	_____
_____	Flashlight	_____	_____
_____	Batteries	_____	_____
_____	Candles	_____	_____
_____	Insect Repellent	_____	_____
_____	Toilet Paper	_____	_____
_____	Trowel	_____	_____
_____	Garbage Bags	_____	_____
_____	Plastic Bags	_____	_____
Canoes			
_____	Canoe	_____	_____
_____	Painters (ropes)	_____	_____
_____	Paddle	_____	_____
_____	Lifejacket	_____	_____
Accommodation			
_____	Tent	_____	_____
_____	Fly	_____	_____
_____	Sleeping Bag	_____	_____
_____	Liner	_____	_____
_____	Underpadding	_____	_____
_____	Plastic Sheet	_____	_____
_____	Tarpaulin	_____	_____

Care of equipment

Canoes

Carefully inspect your canoe for holes or cracks before heading out. Reinforced tape will repair small punctures that may occur during a trip.

At home, fibreglass canoes can be repaired with a kit containing fibreglass cloth, resin and a catalyst. If your canoe is made of polyester resin, your kit should include polyester resin. If made of epoxy, buy a kit with epoxy resin.

Dents in aluminum canoes can be repaired by holding a block of wood against the dented side and carefully pounding on the bulged side with a mallet. Small holes can be sealed with a liquid aluminum compound. Larger holes should have a patch riveted over the hole. If you haven't had experience in riveting, it's best to ask your retailer for his suggestions. Don't try to mend your canoe by welding because this process fatigues the metal.

Small tears in the canvas of cedar-strip canoes can be repaired with waterproof liquid cement. The damaged spot should be dry. Fill the tear with liquid cement and allow it to dry. Apply a second coat. The interior of a cedar-strip canoe needs to be varnished period-ically. Touch it up before each summer.

During the winter, your canoe should be turned over and allowed to rest evenly on four points so that it won't warp. Fibreglass and cedar-strip canoes must also be protected from winter precipitation. If water seeps under the outer layer of a fibreglass canoe or under the canvas of a cedar-strip one, then freezes and expands, it will damage the exterior coating.

Paddles

If the tip of your paddle is wearing, sand it clean and put a fibreglass patch over it. If the paddle's finish is wearing, use Marine Spar Varnish to refinish it. Paddles should be hung up for the winter to prevent warping.

Packs

Packs need to be thoroughly dried out after every use.

Sleeping Bag

If your sleeping bag becomes soiled, take it to a dry cleaner with experience in cleaning sleeping bags. Bags should be hung up when stored. If the insulation is compressed for long periods, it loses its ability to loft up again.

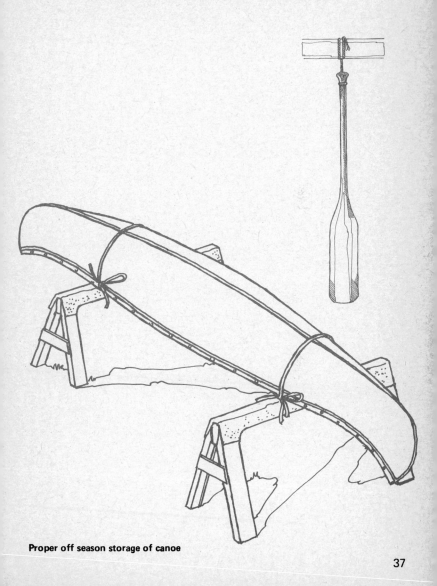

Proper off season storage of canoe

Clothing and personal gear

Clothing needs for canoeing are dictated by comfort, practicality and safety, rather than fashion. You will soon find your own favourite "grubbies" that can take the abuse of a canoe trip. You can experience hot sun, cold rain, muddy portages, snagging brambles, and of course, insects. Appropriate clothing can make the difference between bliss and misery.

You cannot take a lot of clothing on a canoe trip because of its weight and bulk. So, try to make items multi-purpose. Think how you can layer every piece of clothing for the coldest morning rather than taking a heavy coat you may never use. Layering also means that as the day warms up, you can strip down bit by bit.

Some Aspects to Consider

Colour-Light colours are cooler in the sun. Insects are attracted to reds, dark blues, and dark greens.

Fibre-Experienced campers wear wool - socks, sweaters, and long underwear. It is absorbent, and warmer when wet than any other material. Cotton is comfortable next to the body too. Both cotton and wool "breathe" well. Synthetics, on the other hand, trap perspiration and leave you too hot or clammy cold.

Weave-Avoid knits for outer clothing because they catch and snag easily and mosquitoes can bite through them. A tightly woven fabric is best for shirt, jacket, and slacks.

Fit-Loose fitting clothing is more comfortable and allows freer movement and ventilation. Again, mosquitoes can easily bite through tight clothing.

What to Take

Quantities depend on season and length of trip:

• Underwear (cotton or wool) - synthetics are uncomfortable.

• Socks - wool or wool and synthetic blend. Long enough so that pant legs can be tucked into socks when you are in a muddy area or when the bugs are bad. (Black flies love to crawl in around cuffs, collars, and neck openings).

• Slacks - closely woven, loose fit, light colour. Beige workman's trousers or those baggy army surplus pants are great. Avoid wide bell-bottoms that can trip you or catch on sticks. Bluejeans will do if made of tightly woven good quality fabric.

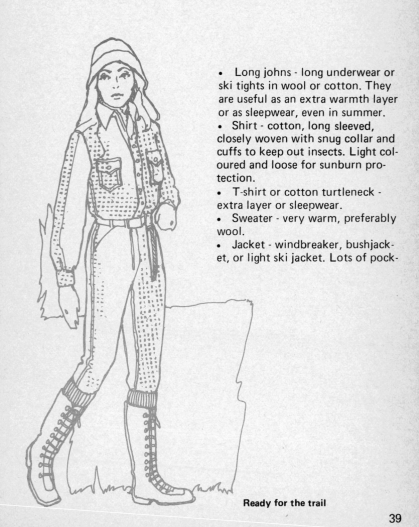

- Long johns - long underwear or ski tights in wool or cotton. They are useful as an extra warmth layer or as sleepwear, even in summer.
- Shirt - cotton, long sleeved, closely woven with snug collar and cuffs to keep out insects. Light coloured and loose for sunburn protection.
- T-shirt or cotton turtleneck - extra layer or sleepwear.
- Sweater - very warm, preferably wool.
- Jacket - windbreaker, bushjacket, or light ski jacket. Lots of pock-

Ready for the trail

ets are handy. A cotton army jacket is ideal.

• Footwear - Canvas sneakers with good non-slip soles are best while in the canoe. However, experienced canoeists planning portages prefer leather hiking boots that come up above the ankle. These give good support and you'll appreciate them when you step into the muddy holes that develop after a rain. Also you can tuck your pants into the higher boots to keep your ankles bug proof. It is very important to protect your feet. You won't be too popular if one of your party has to carry you *and* your pack. Leather boots should be treated with a waterproofing paste before and after each trip. This keeps them pliable as well as water repellent.

• Hat - for protection from the sun and for warmth on cool days. A light coloured and broad brimmed hat is best in the sun. Design a way to tie it on in a stiff wind. Make sure it will fold up and tuck in your pack when it's not needed.

• Bathing suit - comfortable for paddling, should dry quickly.

• Rainwear - The problem of suitable rainwear for a canoe trip has not been solved. Waterproof garments don't breathe so you get wet from your own perspiration - but at least you stay warmer than with no rainwear at all. A light weight rubberized nylon rainsuit costs about $13, and has two pieces; a hooded jacket and pants. Look for one with lots of ventilating flaps. Some people prefer ponchos but they blow in the wind and water runs up your arms as you paddle.

The list opposite can be photocopied and used for each outing. Fill in the quantity of each item that you will need. Check off as you pack. Many of these items are essential to your comfort and safety. Others are obviously frills. Remember, once you have paddled away from the dock none of your belongings can be replaced if lost or damaged. You are on your own.

Pack carefully. Consider the consequences of getting everything wet and guard against it. A small pack lined with a couple of plastic garbage bags should hold all your personal gear. You will be wearing some of the clothing, of course, so it doesn't have to all go in the pack at once.

Personal gear checklist

Check	No. of each Item	
_____	_____	underwear
_____	_____	socks
_____	_____	slacks or jeans
_____	_____	long johns
_____	_____	shirt
_____	_____	T-shirt
_____	_____	sweater
_____	_____	jacket
_____	_____	sneakers
_____	_____	leather boots
_____	_____	brimmed hat
_____	_____	bathing suit
_____	_____	rainwear
_____	_____	belt
_____	_____	knife and sheath
_____	_____	sunglasses
_____	_____	prescription glasses
_____	_____	headband for glasses
_____	_____	flashlight and batteries
_____	_____	insect repellent
_____	_____	matches in water-proof container
_____	_____	watch
_____	_____	camera and film
_____	_____	binoculars
_____	_____	towel and wash-cloth
_____	_____	soap
_____	_____	brush and comb
_____	_____	toothpaste
_____	_____	razor and blades

Check	No. of each Item	
_____	_____	shampoo
_____	_____	lip balm
_____	_____	sunburn cream
_____	_____	small packets of Kleenex
_____	_____	adhesive tape and bandaids
_____	_____	safety pins
_____	_____	elastic bands
_____	_____	garbage bags to line pack
_____	_____	assorted plastic bags
_____	_____	sanitary napkins or tampons
_____	_____	personal medication e.g. hay fever pills
_____	_____	tobacco
_____	_____	notebook and pencil
_____	_____	playing cards
_____	_____	paperback book
_____	_____	reference books e.g. birds or wild flowers
_____	_____	compass
_____	_____	fishing gear
_____	_____	bandana or hand-kerchief
_____	_____	gloves or mittens
_____	_____	warm wooly hat or toque
_____	_____	sleepwear

Camping food

Planning the food for a canoe trip takes time and common sense. An overnight trip for two people is easy. Start on a small scale and do some experimenting. Food planning becomes more complex on longer trips or with larger groups. Your choice of food will reflect your basic canoeing philosophy. Canoeists who enjoy covering huge distances in a day often munch cold snacks rather than take the time to cook a meal. Most of us prefer a more leisurely pace with time to prepare lots of good food over an open fire. Take things you like, try your own ideas - it's fun.

Planning the Menu

Plan a detailed menu for each meal of every day of the trip. You can include fresh foods for the first day or so. Look over the route plan and consider the type of activity for each day. For instance, after a day with heavy portages, dinner should be hearty and quick to prepare.

Be flexible, you will want to rearrange meals according to mood, weather, and changes in plan.

Take along emergency food. A stiff wind could put you behind schedule several days.

Aspects to Consider

• Spoiling - Think how long each item will travel without spoiling. Remember, your food pack gets hot in the sun. Things that melt and run make a mess.

• Weight - Food is surprisingly heavy and much of the weight is water. Freeze-dried foods, which have most of the water extracted, are the ultimate in lightweight camping fare, but they're expensive. Canned foods are much cheaper but very heavy. Consider the amount of portaging on your trip and make your own compromises.

• Nutrition - Take hearty portions of high energy food. Besides burning lots of calories, you also need protein to build muscle - meats, cheese, powdered milk.

• Crushability - Contents of packs get crushed. Crackers crumble and lids pop off plastic containers. Forget glass. It's best to leave anything crushable or breakable at home.

• Garbage - Minimize the amount of non-burnable garbage generated by your food packaging. Paper and plastic wrappings will burn in the campfire, but cans and tinfoil lined packaging will not. Many people just don't take cans, but if you do, burn them on the fire to remove any odour, then flatten them and take them home with you. After the fire dies, pick out any foil that did not burn and take it too. *Burying garbage or dumping it in the lake just isn't acceptable any more.*

Where to Shop

Most of your food shopping can be done at the supermarket. The European delicatessen is also a great resource for the canoeist because of its specialty products - so take a good look around a deli before planning your menu.

Most sporting goods stores have a wide variety of specially packaged freeze-dried foods. You could buy all your food there. It is convenient but *expensive.* Don't be fooled into buying unnecessary items. For instance, freeze-dried pancake mix is no different from the supermarket variety except that it costs more. On the other hand, instant syrup mix is really worth buying at the camping store.

Sample Menu

Below is a possible day's menu for anytime after the third day of a trip. (You could use fresh foods for the first couple of days.) Everything suggested here travels well and and can stay unrefrigerated for a week or two. Each item in the menu has a letter after it to indicate where you can buy it:

S-supermarket   **D**-delicatessen
C-camping specialty store

Breakfast
• Instant orange juice crystals **S**
• Smoked cured bacon in a slab **D** Cut slices off slab each day. Heavy but delicious. To package, wrap in cloth wrung in vinegar, then in plastic bags. Ham is also available.
• Biscuits **S** - Biscuit mix made up with powdered milk. Cook in frying pan or reflector oven.
• Jam, honey, peanut butter **S** - Car-

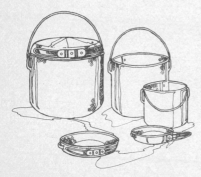

Cooking pots that stack, pack efficiently

43

Camping food

ry in refillable plastic tubes available at camping stores. Carry where tubes won't get squashed.
• Margarine **S** - Don't buy the soft type, it only gets softer out of refrigeration.
• Coffee/tea, cocoa mix, coffee creamer, sugar, powdered milk, salt/pepper, spices **S** - These will be needed at each meal so pack them together. A workman's plastic lunch box is a handy way to organize a lot of small plastic bags. It can also safely hold the few crushables like the plastic tubes and perhaps a plastic bottle of brandy.

Mid-Morning Snack
Handful of granola cereal and some dried fruit (dates, apricots, prunes).

Lunch
If you omit the soup this can be a cold meal - very quick to prepare.
• Rye bread-heavy unsliced loaf **D** - Some kinds keep up to two weeks and don't crush easily.
• Salami **D** - Ask for "dry sausage". It is the type that hangs from hooks unrefrigerated in the delicatessen, and keeps indefinitely. Package the same way as bacon.
• Cheese **S** - Buy it packaged in vacuum-sealed plastic packs.
• Soup **S** or **D** - Dry soup mix

• Freshie or Kool Aid **S**
• Caramels or fudge **S**

Afternoon Snack
A great refuelling snack is a mixture of peanuts, raisins, shredded coconut, and chocolate chips.

Dinner
Stop early enough to do your cooking in the daylight.
• Freeze-dried chicken chunks **C** - Cardboard-like chips that reconstitute in water into tasty chicken. The chicken is expensive but by buying your own rice and sauce you can save some money. Doing it this way is much cheaper than buying a complete instant "chicken and rice dinner."
• Curry sauce mix **D** - There are many Swiss sauce and soup mixes that can be combined with freeze-dried meats to make good meals.
• Rice or noodles **S**
• Freeze-dried peas **C** or **S** - Freeze-dried vegetables are tasty and nutritious and well worth the price.
• Instant chocolate pudding **S** - Can be made with powdered milk and beaten with a fork.

Buying the Food and Packing Up to Go
Before going shopping, decide how

much of each item to buy. Work from your menu to make a list with exact quantities. Be generous. The hardest quantities to decide on will be staples like powdered milk, margarine, sugar, etc.

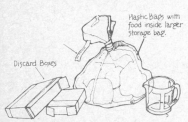

Discard Boxes

Plastic Bags with food inside larger storage bag.

Once home from shopping, the repackaging of the food begins. Experienced canoe trippers get rid of cardboard packaging and measure out each item into plastic bags. Cardboard boxes crush, leak, take up space and their corners puncture other bags.

Remember to take package directions with you. Improvising without a recipe can be fun and some tasty concoctions have evolved as a result. However, sometimes it just doesn't work.

Be prepared for torrential rains or a tipped canoe by wrapping everything in plastic bags inside more plastic bags. This keeps the food dry and minimizes scents that can attract hungry animals. Squeeze all the air out of the bags before sealing or they will pop under pressure in the pack. Wrap the twist ties flat so they don't puncture the bags.

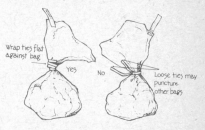

Wrap ties flat against bag

Yes

No

Loose ties may puncture other bags

Putting all the food in one pack means you have only one pack to hang out of reach of the animals each night (see page 48). Line this pack with two big garbage bags. Some thought while packing will make it easier to find things during the trip. Food to be eaten late in the trip should be stored at the bottom. Some canoeists put all the bagged items for one meal in a larger bag and label it (e.g. *Tuesday Dinner - Spaghetti*). Things needed at each meal go in last (salt, tea, margarine) so that they are easily accessible.

Before setting off on your adventure, check that you have a copy of your menu and all recipes.

Safety and planning

Route Planning

Topographical maps, most costing $1.00, are invaluable in route planning and on the trip. Those with a scale of 1:50,000 (i.e. 1.27 inches on the map equal to one mile on the ground) give the best detail. "Top" maps clearly indicate bodies of water and most portages. Contour lines graphically interpret the elevations of the area. Rapids and falls are shown, as well as marshes, bogs and woodland. By noting the water levels of two connected lakes you know that the river flows toward the one with the lowest level. Also along the map margin is compass declination and a map legend. To find out what "top" maps are available in Ontario, get the free map index from the Provincial Government Map Office, (you can order this with the tear out page). Once you have the map index, you can then order the specific maps you need.

If you can, go directly to the provincial map office. Located on the sixth floor of the Whitney Block of the Parliament Buildings, at the corner of Wellesley and Queen's Park Crescent, in Toronto, 416-965-6511, it's well worth a visit. Once you have your "top" maps,

you can make a daily route plan.

How Far to Paddle

When you go canoeing in new areas, temper that sense of adventure with a good dose of caution. Don't make the mistake of heading 15 miles downstream and remembering, as the sun starts to set, that you have to get back to your car. Plan to paddle no more than ten miles on your first full day outing, and if you're going overnight, set up camp early to utilize the daylight hours. Also take into account the time and energy that you will be expending on portages. If you plan more than three portages in a day, don't expect to cover many water miles. Break your trip often for snacks - you canoe to enjoy yourself, not to set endurance records. And, if you decide to tackle something more ambitious than a weekend, exercise regularly beforehand. The more physically fit you are, the more you'll enjoy canoe-tripping.

First Aid

Being outdoors all day has its special problems. The sun is a joy to feel on your back, but be careful. Its rays, coupled with the water's reflection, can cause a bad sunburn. Expose your skin gradually to the sun, and wear a hat. If you are particularly susceptible to the sun, apply cream that blocks out the sun's rays entirely. On hot days, if you seem to have an insatiable thirst for water, your body is telling you that it needs salt. (Salt pills are inexpensive and available at any drugstore.)

Blisters mark the beginning of the canoeing season. At first signs of a blister, cover it with a band-aid. Don't attempt to break it.

Of course, anyone with a medical problem like an allergy or epilepsy should inform the others in his party.

It is wise for someone in your canoeing party to have first aid training (St. John Ambulance offer a good course).

Dangerous Waters

Venturing out into large bodies of water can be risky for any canoeist, let alone the inexperienced. Sudden storms also mean trouble. Always try to skirt the shoreline of large lakes, but if you're offshore and the wind starts to blow up, point either your bow or stern into the waves so water doesn't splash into your canoe. If you're at all worried, make sure you're in the kneeling position, put on your life jacket and tie it securely.

What do you do if you tip over? If you don't have your life jacket on, and it's at all possible to reach it, put it on and hold onto your canoe. Worry about rescuing the equipment later. If you are fairly close to land, hold on and kick the canoe to shore. Otherwise, hold on and try to attract attention.

Novice canoeists should gain experience on flat water (ponds and lakes). Rivers usually mean currents and can cause problems. Rivers may also mean rapids and waterfalls. It is imperative to have whitewater training before attempting to run rapids. When travelling downstream, it's very difficult to tell whether that drop ahead is simply a little fast water or a waterfall. If you see whitewater ahead or hear any sort of roar, pull over to the river bank. Walk the full length of the fast water and carefully assess it. If you're inexperienced in running rapids or have any doubts, play it safe and portage.

Safety in Numbers

On a canoe trip, it's safer to travel in a party of at least two canoes.

Safety and planning

If one canoe tips or is severely damaged, you can rely upon the people in the other canoes to aid you. On longer trips, experienced canoeists plan a party of at least three canoes. In case of a canoe's loss, paddlers can triple up in the remaining canoes.

Map and Compass

Using a map and compass takes know-how and practice. Make sure you have these skills before entering the wilderness. The object of map reading is to form a true mental picture of the ground. A good way to start learning is to read the government publication called *Everybody Should Be Able to Use a Map* available at the Provincial Government's Map Office (use the tear out at the back of this book to order it). An excellent book on finding your way through wilderness areas is Calvin Rustrum's *Wilderness Route Finder* (see page 78). For those of you who want to hone your map reading skills, join the Ontario Orienteering Association, 559 Jarvis St., Toronto, 416-964-8655.

If You Get Lost or Injured

Not learning how to read a map

can have immediate consequences . . . getting lost!
In most of southern Ontario, civilization is nearby. However, in the central and northern areas, you are more isolated and could become quite lost. Before leaving on any trip, tell somebody where you are going and when you plan to return.
If you do get lost or injured, stop moving. Find yourself an open space, wait, and make yourself comfortable. Attract the attention of a passer-by, or signal to aircraft with a reflecting surface. Three fires in a triangle about 50 feet apart are a recognized signal of distress. Don't attempt to travel in the dark.

Drinking Water

Unfortunately, many rivers and lakes in Ontario are polluted. If you have any doubts about water quality, it's best to take tap water. You can purify mildly polluted lakewater with halazone tablets or a disinfectant. Halazone is available at most drugstores. Household chlorine bleach also works effectively. Simply put six drops into a gallon of water and wait 20 minutes.

Animals

In more civilized areas, such furry

48

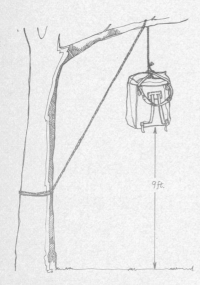

9 ft.

comes a pest and a possible danger. In many parks these nuisance bears must be shot. Feeding a bear can have the same effect as pulling the trigger of the rifle that eventually has to shoot it.

Poison Ivy

Poison Ivy is common to central Ontario. The oil or juice of this little plant is an irritant to the skin which produces a rash and blisters, along with considerable discomfort. If you suspect contact with the plant, wash the area thoroughly with hot water and soap and then wash off with rubbing alcohol. Learning to recognize the plant is the best protection.

animals as bears and racoons have lost their natural fear of man. They've come to realize that man is a potential pushover for a meal and consequently think nothing of raiding campsites. For this reason, hang your food pack from a tree limb at least nine feet off the ground. If car camping, it's easier to put your food in your car. Don't feed bears or leave them edible garbage. Once a bear learns that humans are a source of food, it be-

49

Protecting the environment

Old time woodsmen lived off the land; building shelters, cutting bough beds, burying their garbage. There were few of them and the land recovered between their infrequent visits. Our wilderness can no longer stand these old-fashioned practices. There are now so many of us that each person must minimize his own effect on the wild country he visits.

Litter

There is an amazing amount of garbage strewn along our canoe routes - ugly evidence that you are not the first to travel the wilderness paths.

Carry out all your empty containers (insect repellent bottles, empty cans, etc.) Burn paper and plastic. Look around each campsite before leaving. Even a shirt put to dry on a limb becomes litter once it is left behind.

Campfires

Fires are safest built on bare rock. In areas with humus soil and tree roots, your campfire can spread underground without detection. Careful campers dig down to mineral soil before lighting a fire. You may have to travel some distance from camp to find good wood. Look for small dead trees

still standing. Don't cut live wood - - it won't burn anyway.

Before leaving camp double check that the fire is dead. To put out the fire stir in water until the coals are cold to the touch.

Smoking

Smoking in the woods requires special caution. Always stop and sit to have your smoke. Account for each cold match and butt before moving on.

Toilets

Carry a trowel or folding shovel to dig a latrine (well back from camp and at least 100 feet from shore). Fill it in before you leave that site.

Water Pollution

As well as keeping your sewage away from the water, think about your soaps and detergents. Look for biodegradable products. Dump soapy water on the soil well back from the shore.

Barren Campsites

Old-fashioned practices (cutting tentpoles and bough beds, building shelters and tables) are denuding many campsites. Digging of new fireplaces or ditches around tents contributes to erosion. Large groups trample vegetation.

Algonquin and Killarney Provincial Parks

Algonquin Park spreads over 2,910 square miles of the southern edge of the rocky Canadian Shield. In this park, crystal clear water surrounded by rugged granite rocks and evergreens permits canoe travel in almost any direction. The canoeist awakens to the cry of the loon, and the morning sun burning the mist off the lake. If you are planning a trip in Algonquin, the 'Algonquin Provincial Park Canoe Routes' brochure is a must. Use the tear-out page at back of book to order it.

Killarney Park also offers spectacular canoeing adventures. Located at the northern end of Georgian Bay, the park spreads over a series of quartzite mountains. These eroded white mountains plunge deeply into the waters of the area, turning the lakes into a fantasy of aquamarine. A series of rivers and lakes allow access to Georgian Bay. For more information contact the Killarney Provincial Park District Manager, Ministry of Natural Resources, 174 Douglas St. W., Sudbury, P3E 1G1. 705-673-1111.

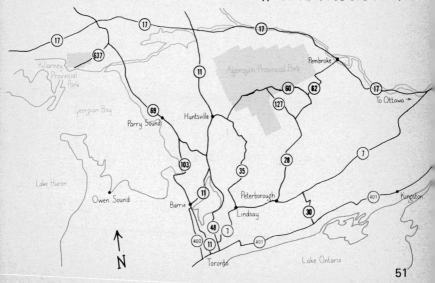

Where to canoe in Southern and Central Ontario

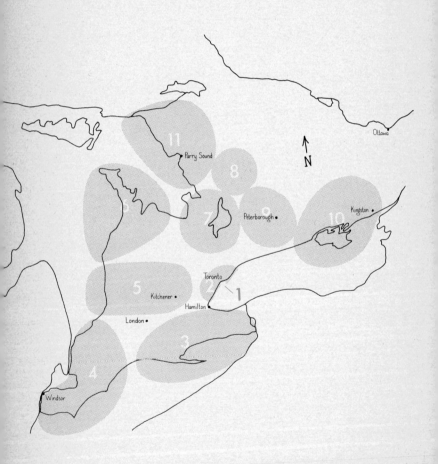

You can canoe in virtually any water deeper than six inches. In this section, we recommend areas mostly suited to day and weekend outings. The map opposite divides Ontario into eleven regions and on the twenty-two pages which follow, there are detailed maps of each region. The numbers indicate areas to canoe, of which there are two sorts: those in supervised areas like provincial parks and conservation areas, and those waterways under no particular jurisdiction. The former are excellent for novices who want to enjoy canoeing in safe surroundings. The latter require more experience and wilderness skills. Maps of both provincial parks and conservation areas can be ordered with the tear-out at the back of the book. The section on 'Safety and Planning' (page 46) will help you realize some of the potential problems.

Each listing, whenever possible, has an address and telephone number to contact for more information. The legend indicates available restaurants, stores, instruction, canoe rentals, washrooms, car camping, low water in summer, or overnight canoe camping. Overnight canoe camping means there are overnight tenting spots to which you may paddle. To get to any of these areas, take along a good road map.

Don't feel restricted to the listings in this book. Half the fun of canoeing is finding out what is beyond the next bend, or exploring the mouth of a different river. Remember, however that most land in south and central Ontario is privately owned. If you want to camp on private land, ask the owner for permission. Of course, leave the site cleaner than when you arrived, so the next canoeists who ask for permission will not be refused.

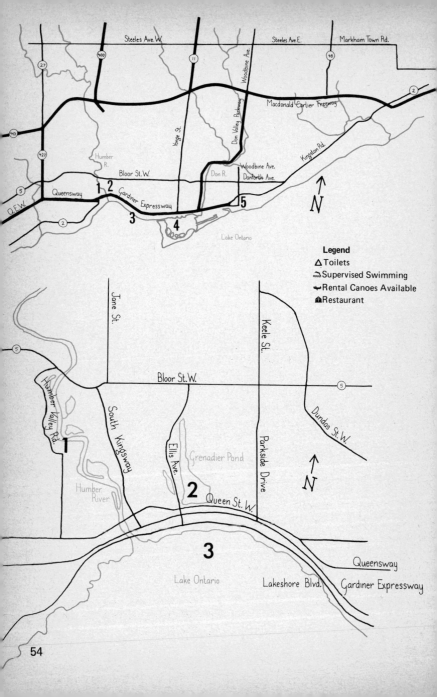

Legend

△ Toilets
⌒ Supervised Swimming
✈ Rental Canoes Available
🏠 Restaurant

1
Toronto Region

There are five areas right in Metro Toronto suitable for a day's canoe outing. On a calm summer's day, you can enjoy Lake Ontario if you have your own equipment, or the crowded waterways of Toronto Island in a rented canoe, without ever leaving the city.

1 Humber River
Access from Humber Valley Rd. S. of Hwy. 5.
During summer you can paddle from the Old Mill Bridge to Lake Ontario. Canoeing free.

2 Grenadier Pond
From Queen St. West westbound, turn N. on Ellis Ave. Car parking on the street.
Use your own canoe or rent one from High Park Boat Rentals. 416-766-9787. Canoeing free.
△ ⌣ 🏠

3 Lakeshore Boulevard Area
From Lakeshore Blvd. W., eastbound turn right into Sir Casmir Gzowski Park, Budapest Park or into the parking lot just east of Toronto Sailing Club. Parking spaces fill quickly on hot days.
Canoe on the shore side of the breakwall. Canoeing free.
△ 🏠

4 Toronto Island
Take the Centre Island or the Ward's Island ferry from the foot of Bay St. 416-367-8193 for the timetable.
The canoe rental concession run by John Jain is on Centre Island. Open all summer daily from 10 a.m. to sunset. 416-864-1666.
△ ⌣ 🏠

5 Beaches
From Lakeshore Drive E., turn right onto Kew Beach Ave. Parking on the street.
Lake Ontario is suitable for canoeing only on calm days. Canoeing free.
△ ⌐ 🏠

Toronto Canoe Outfitters
These marinas will rent canoes, paddles and lifejackets for approximately $8. a day.

All-Season's Marine, 3035 Dufferin St. Toronto, M6B 3T7. 416-782-3623.

Irwin Marine, 1649 Weston Rd. Weston, M9N 1V2. 416-248-6217.

Kennedy Boats, 1153 Kennedy Rd. Scarborough, M1P 2K8. 416-757-1234

Reerie's Bait (supplies roof rack for some auto makes) 4659 Kingston Rd. Scarborough, M1E 2P8. 416-282-5876.

2 Toronto Suburban Region

1 Mountsberg Conservation Area. From Campbellville, turn S.W. onto Campbellville Rd. Go to the third sideroad, and turn N.W. for ½ mi. to the park. 416-854-2741. For more information contact Halton Region Conservation Authority, 310 Main St. Milton, L9T 1P4.

600 acre reservoir in 1120 acre area. Charge, $2.00 per car. No overnight camping.

●△🏠⊙

2 Kelso Conservation Area. From Hwy 401, take Hwy 25 S. to Baseline Rd.

Legend

● No Power Boats
□ Instruction
△ Toilets
✳ Store
� Supervised Swimming

▼ Low Water In Summer
🛶 Rental Canoes Available
🏠 Restaurant
▲ Car Camping
⊙ Fireplaces
🛶Overnight Canoe Camping

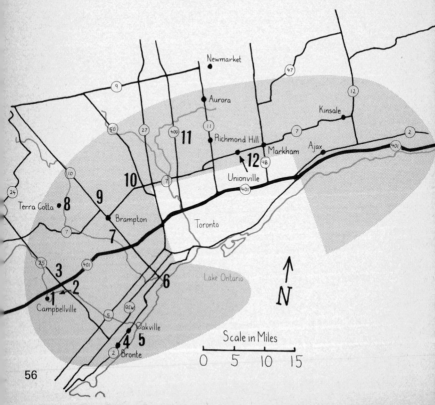

Scale in Miles

0   5   10   15

N

Turn S.W. 1 mi., then N.
W. 1½ mi. on second line
Esquesing Township, and
S.W. 2 mi. through Milton
Heights to park. 416-878-
4476. For more informa-
tion contact Halton Reg-
ion Conservation Author-
ity, 310 Main St. Milton.
L9T 1P4

80 acre reservoir for ca-
noeing in 381 acre area.
Charge, $2.00 per car,
$1.00 per person for over-
night camping.

●△⌂⌂▲☉

**3 Scotch Block Conserva-
tion Area.** Located on
Hwy. 25, 3 mi. N. of Hwy.
401. For more informa-
tion contact Halton Reg-
ion Conservation Author-
ity, 310 Main St., Milton,
L9T 1P4. 416-878-4131.

80 acre reservoir for ca-
noeing in a 124 acre area.
Day use free. No over-
night camping.

●

4 Bronte Creek. Access to
creek from Hwy 2 in
Bronte.

River is twisting, navig-
able for about 2 mi. up-
stream from its mouth in
the summer. Day use free.
No overnight camping.

5 Oakville Creek. Access
from Hwy 2 in Oakville.

Creek allows for a winding
trip of some 2.3 mi. up
river from the harbour.
Motor boats are restricted
to 5 mph. Day use free. No
overnight camping.

6 Credit River. From the
QEW, go S. on Hwy. 10,

turn W. at Mineola Rd.
and follow road to end.

River offers about 5 mi.
canoeing. Excellent place
to see bird life and autumn
leaves. Day use free. No
overnight camping.

**7 Meadowvale Conserva-
tion Area.** From Hwy 10,
north of 401, turn W. at
Derry Rd. West. Meadow-
vale is 2 mi. W. of No. 10.
Conservation Area is on
westerly limits of Meadowvale, For further information contact Credit Valley
Conservation Authority,
Meadowvale, L0J 1K0.
416-451-1615.

Canoeing on Credit River.
Charge, $2.00 per car. No
overnight camping.

●△☉

**8 Terra Cotta Conserva-
tion Area.** From Terra
Cotta, go 1 mi. N. to en-
trance. For more informa-
tion contact Credit Valley
Conservation Authority,
Meadowvale, L0J 1K0.
416-451-1615.

Canoeing on a 6 acre pond.
Charge, $1.50 per car,
$2.50 per night.

●△⌂⌂▲☉

**9 Heart Lake Conservation
Area.** Go 4 mi. N. of Hwy
7 on the Second Line. For
more information contact
Metro Toronto and Region
Conservation Authority,
5 Shoreham Dr., Downs-
view, M3N 2S6. 416-630-
9780.

Canoeing on a small lake.
Charge, $1.75 per car,
$2.00 per night.

●⌂▲☉

**10 Clairville Conservation
Area.** Located on Hwy 7,
1 mi. W. of Hwy 50. For
more information contact
Metro Toronto and Region
Conservation Authority,
5 Shoreham Dr., Downs-
view, M3N 2S6. 416-630-
9780.

Canoeing on a 120 acre
pond. Charge, $1.50 per
car, $5.00 overnight.

●△⌂⌂▲☉▲♦

11 Seneca College. From
Hwy 400 go E. on King
City Sideroad and N. on
Dufferin St. Seneca Col-
lege is on the west side.
For more information
contact Seneca College,
Dufferin St. N. R.R. #3,
King City, L0G 1K0. 416-
884-9901.

Seneca has a large lake on
646 acres of wooded park-
land and offers beginner,
intermediate and advanced
canoeing courses starting
in the spring. Canoes may
be rented but reservations
are necessary. *No private
canoes allowed.* Also available, courses in building
your own canoe, making
your own camping equip-
ment and wilderness ad-
venture training.

●□△↩⌂

12 Rouge River. Access
from Hwy 7, just east of
Unionville.

Water level is controlled
by a dam. When the water
is high, it's possible to paddle to Markham and back,
a distance of about 6 mi.,
through a variety of wooded and flooded pastoral
terrain. Canoeing free. No
overnight camping.

3 Niagara Region

1 Big Otter Creek. From Hwy 19, turn W. at Eden onto County Rd. 44. Big Otter Creek runs under County Rd. 44. *Big Otter Creek* brochure, available from the Long Point Region Conservation Authority, Box 525, Simcoe, N3Y 4W5. 519-426-4623.

20 mi. of river flowing to Lake Erie. River can dry up during drought periods. Canoeing free. Overnight camping with permission of the land owner.

▼⚲♨

2 Iroquois Provincial Park. Go south from Tillson-

Legend
● No Power Boats
□ Instruction
△ Toilets
✳ Store
⊃ Supervised Swimming

▼ Low Water In Summer
↜ Rental Canoes Available
🏠 Restaurant
▲ Car Camping
⊙ Fireplaces
♨ Overnight Canoe Camping

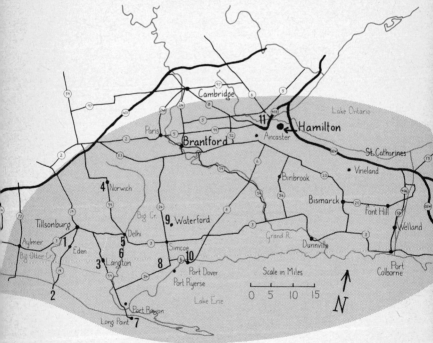

burg on Hwy 19. For more information contact Ministry of Natural Resources, 353 Talbot St. W., Aylmer, N5H 1K5. 519-773-9241.

Canoeing on the Big Otter Creek, and on Lake Erie on calm days. Charge, $1.50 per car, $3.50 overnight.

△▲⊙

3 Deer Creek Conservation Area. From Hwy 59 S. of Langton, turn W. onto County Rd. 45. Follow it to the park. For more information contact Long Point Region Conservation Authority, Box 525, Simcoe, N3Y 4W5. 519-875-2874.

Area has 200 acres of picturesque woodlands, valleys and gullies and a 76 acre lake. Charge, $1.50 per car, $3.50 overnight.

●△▲⊙

4 Norwich Dam. From Hwy 59 in Norwich, turn W. on Main St. and, N. on Clyde St. For more information contact Long Point Region Conservation Authority, Box 525, Simcoe, N3Y 4W5. 519-426-4623.

A 33 acre lake has been created by the dam. Canoeing free. No overnight camping.

●△

5 Lehman Dam. Located in Delhi, near the intersection of Hwys 3 and 59. For more information contact Long Point Region Conservation Authority, Box 525, Simcoe, N3Y 4W5. 519-426-4623.

Canoeing on a 46 acre water supply reservoir. Canoeing free. No overnight camping.

●

6 Big Creek Canoe Route. Take County Rd. 42 W. from Hwy 59. Access from bridge over Big Creek. For brochure, contact Long Point Region Conservation Authority, Box 525, Simcoe, N3Y 4W5. 519-426-4623.

From this point Big Creek is navigable for 25 mi. to Lake Erie. River can dry up during drought periods. Canoeing free. Overnight camping with permission of the land owner.

▼♣

7 Long Point Provincial Park. From Hwy 3, go S. on Hwy 59 to the end of the road. For more information contact Ministry of Natural Resources, Long Point Provincial Park, Port Rowan, N0E 1M0. 519-586-2133.

Lagoons allow safe canoeing on north side of Long Point. Charge, $1.50 per car, $3.50 overnight.

△✱⌂▲⊙

8 Vittoria Conservation Area. From Hwy 24, turn W. onto Vittoria Rd. Follow Vittoria Rd. W. 1½ mi. to the area. For more information contact Long Point Region Conservation Authority, Box 525, Simcoe, N3Y 4W5. 519-426-4623.

Canoeing on Young Creek. Day use free. No overnight camping.

⊙

9 Waterford Conservation Area. Located on Thompson Rd., just E. of Hwy 24, near Waterford. For more information contact Long Point Conservation Authority, Box 525, Simcoe, N3Y 4W5. 519-426-4623.

Canoeing on 200 acres of lakes converted from gravel pits. Charge $1.50 per car. No overnight camping.

●△⛵⌂

10 Black Creek Conservation Area. From Port Dover, go 1 mi. N. on County Rd. 15, then 3/4 mi. E. on sideroad. For more information contact Long Point Region Conservation Authority, Box 525, Simcoe, N3Y 4W5. 519-426-4623.

Canoeing on Black Creek. Free. No overnight camping.

△

11 Coote's Paradise. From Hwy 403, go E. on Main St. to Dundurn St., go N. to King St., then turn W. Follow King St. over bridge to Longwood St. Turn N. and take road to the end (Princess Point). For more information contact Royal Botanical Gardens, 680 Plains Rd. W., Burlington. 416-527-1158.

1 sq. mi. of canoeing area and access to canal that goes into Dundas. Canoeing free.

●△↩⊙

4 South West Region

1 Running Creek Conservation Area. Access from Forham St. in Wallaceburg. For more information contact St. Clair Region Conservation Authority, 205 Front St. E., Strathroy, N7G 1Y8. 519-626-1223.

Canoeing on Sydenham River. Day use free. No overnight camping.

●△☉

2 Thames River. Access from Thames St., S. off Grant St. in Chatham.

River is navigable for 20 mi. downstream to Lake

Legend

- ● No Power Boats
- ▢ Instruction
- △ Toilets
- ✳ Store
- ⌣ Supervised Swimming
- ▼ Low Water In Summer
- ↰ Rental Canoes Available
- 🏠 Restaurant
- ▲ Car Camping
- ☉ Fireplaces
- ▲● Overnight Canoe Camping

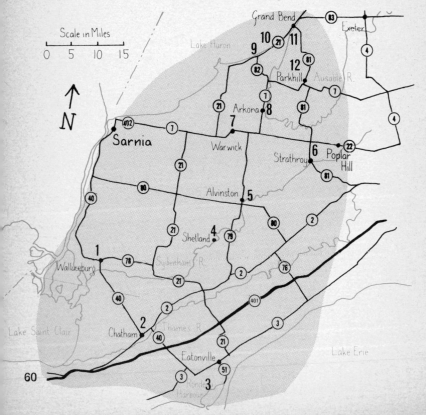

Scale in Miles

0   5   10   15

N

St. Clair, and upstream to London. Day use free. No overnight camping.

3 Rondeau Provincial Park. From Hwy 3, turn S. at Eatonville onto Hwy 51. Follow it to the park. For more information, contact Ministry of Natural Resources, 353 Talbot St. W., Aylmer, N5H 1K5. 519-773-9241.

Canoeing in Rondeau Harbour. Charge, $1.50 per car, $3.50 overnight.

△✳▲

4 Shetland Conservation Area. From Shetland, go ½ mi. N. on County Rd. 8. For more information contact St. Clair Region Conservation Authority, 205 Front St. E., Strathroy, N7G 1Y8. 519-695-5437.

Canoeing on Sydenham River. Day use free. Charge, $3.00 per car overnight.

△▲⊙⚌

5 A.W. Campbell Conservation Area. Go E. for 2 mi. on first Concession Rd. N. of Alvinston. For more information contact St. Clair Region Conservation Authority, 205 Front St. E., Strathroy, N7G 1Y8. 519-695-5437.

Canoeing on 18 acre lake. Charge $1.00 per car,

●△⇋⊙

6 Strathroy Conservation Area. Access from Head St. in Strathroy. For more information contact St. Clair Region Conservation Authority, 205 Front St.

E., Strathroy, N7G 1Y8. 519-245-3710.

Canoeing on Sydenham River. Instruction available for $6.00 through the Strathroy Canoe Club. Day use free. No overnight camping.

△⊙

7 Warwick Conservation Area. Located on Hwy 7 in the town of Warwick. For more information contact St. Clair Region Conservation Authority, 205 Front St., Strathroy, N7G 1Y8. 519-876-6081.

Canoeing on Bear Creek. Charge, $1.00 per car, $3.00 overnight.

●△⇋▲⊙

8 Rock Glen Conservation Area. From Hwy 7 in the village of Arkona, go 3/4 mi. E. on Rock Glen Rd. For more information contact Ausable-Bayfield Conservation Authority, Box 459, Exeter, N0M 1S0. 519-235-2610.

Canoeing on Ausable River. Charge, $1.00 per car, no overnight camping.

△⊙

9 Port Franks Conservation Area. Go 2 mi. N.W. of intersection of Hwy 21 and Hwy 82. For more information contact Ausable-Bayfield Conservation Authority, Box 459, Exeter, N0M 1S0. 519-235-2610.

Canoeing on Ausable River Cut. Day use free. No overnight camping.

△⊙

10 Thedford Conservation Area. From the intersec-

tion of Hwys 21 and 82, go N.E. 1 mi. on 21. Area is on W. side. For more information contact Ausable-Bayfield Conservation Authority, Box #459, Exeter, N0M 1S0. 519-235-2610.

Canoeing on Ausable River Cut. Charge, 50¢ per car, No overnight camping.

△⊙

11 Ausable River. Access at Pinery Provincial Park, 5 mi. S. of Grand Bend on Hwy 21. For more information contact Superintendent, Pinery Provincial Park. R.R. #2, Grand Bend, N0M 1T0. 519-243-2220.

There are guided canoe trips by the Pinery staff in the summer. Park has sand dune terrain covered by pine, oak, hickory, poplar, birch and cherry. Charge, $1.50 per car, $3.50 overnight.

△⇋▲⊙

12 Parkhill Conservation Area. Go directly N. of Parkhill at intersection of Hwys 7 and 81. For more information contact Ausable-Bayfield Conservation Authority, Box 459, Exeter, N0M 1S0. 519-235-2610.

Lake available for canoeing. Charge, $1.00 per car, $3.50 overnight.

●△✳↵⊙

5 Kitchener Region

1 Morrison Dam. From junction of Hwy 4 and Hwy 83, go E. for 1¼ mi., then S. on gravel rd. for ½ mi. For more information contact Ausable-Bayfield Conservation Authority, Box 459, Exeter, N0M 1S0. 519-235-2610.

Canoeing on 35 acre lake created by a dam. Day use free. No overnight camping.

●▲⊙

2 Bayfield River. From Varna, go N. of Hwy 31 to Bayfield R. In the spring you may also start at Egmondville, just S. of Sea-

Legend
- ● No Power Boats
- □ Instruction
- △ Toilets
- ✳ Store
- ⌣ Supervised Swimming
- ▼ Low Water In Summer
- ⌐ Rental Canoes Available
- ♨ Restaurant
- ▲ Car Camping
- ⊙ Fireplaces
- ♨ Overnight Canoe Camping

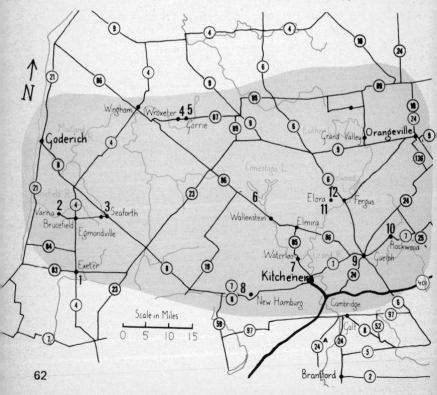

forth on Hwy 8. *Canoe the Bayfield River* brochure available from Ministry of Natural Resources, Box 490, Wingham, N0G 2W0. 519-357-3131.

6 mi. stretch from Varna to Lake Huron on Bayfield River 12 mi. from Egmondville to Varna. Canoeing free. No overnight camping.

3 South Maitland River. From Seaforth on Hwy 8, head N.E. on County Rd. 12. *Canoe The Maitland* brochure available from Ministry of Natural Resources, Box 490, Wingham, N0G 2W0. 519-357-3131.

A 15 mi. route takes you to the main Maitland River. From here, the river flows to Goderich. Canoeing free.

4 Maitland River. Access from Wroxeter on Hwy 87. *Canoe The Maitland* brochure available from Ministry of Natural Resources, Box 490, Wingham, N0G 2W0. 519-357-3131.

40 mi. meandering river flows through farmland to Goderich. Campsites are located along the route. The channel near Auburn has interesting 75-foot stratified clay walls. Canoeing free.

⚲⚲

5 Gorrie Conservation Area. Located in Gorrie on Hwy 87. For more information contact Maitland Valley Conservation Authority, Box 5, Wrox-

eter, N0G 2X0. 519-335-3557.

Canoeing on a 28 acre pond. Day use free. No overnight camping.

△⊙ ●

6 Conestogo Lake Conservation Area. From Elmira, travel N.W. on Hwy 86 to County Rd. 11. Follow County Rd. N. for 2 mi. to park. For more information contact Conestogo Lake Conservation Area. R.R. #1, Wallenstein, N0B 2S0. 519-638-2873.

Conestogo Lake has two 6 mi. arms. Charge, $1.75 per car, $2.00 overnight.

△⌂⌂⚲⊙⚲⚲

7 Laurel Creek Conservation Area. From Waterloo, take Weber St. to Northfield Dr. For more information contact Laurel Creek Conservation Area, R.R. #4, Waterloo. 519-884-6620.

Canoeing on a 250 acre pond. Charge $1.75 per car. $2.00 overnight.

●△⌂⚲⌂⚲

8 W.J. Scott Conservation Area. Located just W. of New Hamburg on Hwy 7/8. For more information contact W.J. Scott Conservation Area, Box 729, Cambridge, or phone Grand River Conservation Authority, 519-621-2761.

Canoeing on the Nith R. Day use free. No overnight camping.

△

9 Silver Creek Conservation Area. Located in Guelph at the corner of

Silver Creek Parkway and Edinborough Rd. For more information contact Silver Creek Conservation Area, Box 729, Cambridge. 519-621-2761.

Canoeing on the Speed River. Day use free. No overnight camping.

●△

10 Rockwood Conservation Area. Located on Hwy 7, just W. of the village of Rockwood. For more information contact Rockwood Conservation Area, Box 60, Rockwood, N0B 2K0. 519-856-9543.

Canoeing on an 18 acre lake and river. Charge, $1.75 per car, $2.00 overnight. ☐

●△⌂⚲⌂⚲⊙

11 Elora Gorge. Located S. of Elora at junction of Hwy 6 and Elora Rd. For more information contact Elora Conservation Area, Elora, N0B 1S0. 519-846-9742.

Canoeing on the Grand River. Charge, $1.75 per car, $2.00 overnight.

●△⌂⌂⚲⊙

12 Grand River — Elora to Lake Erie. Access at Elora off Hwy 6 and at Cambridge, Brantford and Caledonia. *Grand River Canoe Route* brochure available from Ministry of Natural Resources, Box 490, Wingham, N0G 2W0. 519-357-3131.

The Grand River winds through a varied landscape, from rugged, cliff-lined shores to gently rolling farmlands.

▼⚲⚲

6 Bruce Peninsula Region

1 Inverhuron Provincial Park. From Hwy 21 at Tiverton, go W. 4 mi. to Inverhuron. For more information contact Ministry of Natural Resources, 101 Holiday Inn Dr., Hespeler, N3C 1Z3. 519-658-9356.

Canoeing on Lake Huron on calm days. Charge, $1.50 per car, $3.50 overnight.
△▲⊙

2 Brucedale Conservation Area. Go 2½ mi. N. of Underwood on Hwy 21 to Concession Rd. 10, then W. for 3½ mi. to the end

Legend

- ● No Power Boats
- ▢ Instruction
- △ Toilets
- ⚹ Store
- ⌒ Supervised Swimming
- ▼ Low Water In Summer
- ⇀ Rental Canoes Available
- ⌂ Restaurant
- ▲ Car Camping
- ⊙ Fireplaces
- ⚲ Overnight Canoe Camping

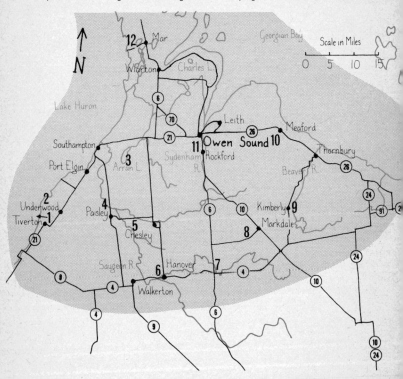

of the road. Park is 1 mi. to the N. For more information contact Saugeen Valley Conservation Authority, R.R. #1, Hanover. N4N 3B8. 519-364-1255.

Canoeing on Lake Huron on calm days. Day use free. Charge, $3.50 overnight.

△▲☉

3 Arran Lake Conservation Area. From Port Elgin, go E. on County Rd. 17. Turn N. on first concession road W. of Arkwright. For more information contact North Grey-Sauble Conservation Authority, 330 Tenth St., Owen Sound, N4K 3R5. 519-376-3076.

Canoeing on Arran Lake. Day use free. No overnight camping.

△☉

4 Saugeen Bluffs Conservation Area. From Paisley, take Bruce City Rd. No. 3 N. 2½ mi. Turn left onto Sideroad 8/9. For more information contact Saugeen Valley Conservation Authority, R.R. #1, Hanover, N4N 3B8. 519-364-1255.

Canoeing on Saugeen River. Day use free. Charge, $3.50 overnight per car.

△▲☉

5 Porter Conservation Area. Go 7 mi. W. of Chesley on Bruce City Rd. 2-3. For more information contact Saugeen Valley Conservation Authority, R.R. #1, Hanover, N4N 3B8. 519-364-1255.

Canoeing on Saugeen River. Day use free. Over-

night camping outside of park.

△

6 Saugeen River. Start at Hanover on Hwy. 4. *Saugeen River Canoe Route* brochure available from Ministry of Natural Resources, 101 Holiday Inn Dr. Hespeler, N3C 1Z3. 519-658-9356.

The river meanders resulting in a water route nearly twice as long as the road route. Banks are heavily treed.

▼▲♀

7 Durham Conservation Area. Go N. on Hwy 6 to Durham Rd. Go E. 1½ mi. on Durham Rd. For more information contact Saugeen Valley Conservation Authority, R.R. #1, Hanover, N4N 3B8. 519-369-2074.

Canoeing on a pond formed by a dam. Charge, $1.00 per car, $3.50 overnight.

△▲☉

8 Bell's Lake Conservation Area. Go 5 mi. W. of Markdale on Grey City Rd. 12. Turn right on sideroad 10/11. Go N. 2 mi. For more information contact Saugeen Valley Conservation Authority, R.R. #1, Hanover, N4N 3B8. 519-364-1255.

Canoeing on a 340 acre lake. Day use free. Charge, $3.50 overnight per car.

△▲☉

9 Beaver River - Kimberley to Thornbury. Access from County Rd. 13 at Kimberley. *Beaver River Canoe*

Route brochure available from Ministry of Natural Resources, 101 Holiday Inn Dr., Hespeler, N3C 1Z3. 519-658-9356.

River flows through a great variety of terrain, from flat fields and forest to craggy limestone cliffs.

▲♀

10 Meaford Conservation Area. Located in Meaford at Junction of Hwy 26 and Grey County Rd. 12. For more information contact North Grey Conservation Authority, 330 Tenth St. W., Owen Sound, N4K 3R5. 519-376-3076.

Canoeing on Bighead River and Georgian Bay. Day use free. No overnight camping.

△☉

11 Harrison Park. Take Hwy 6/10 to Owen Sound. For more information contact Mr. Ed Taylor, Harrison Park, Owen Sound. 519-376-1835.

Park allows access onto Sydenham River flowing into Georgian Bay. YMCA runs a canoe course.

●□△✳⌒♠▲☉

12 Rankin River - Sky Lake to Sauble Falls. Start at Concession Rd. W. of Mar. *Rankin Route* brochure available from Ministry of Natural Resources, Box 490, Wingham, N0G 2W0. 519-357-3131.

This 11 mile river is good for a day trip. The route flows through marshland scenery and jungle-like treed swamps. Day use free.

▲♀

7 Lake Simcoe Region

1 Edenvale Conservation Area. Located on Hwy 26, 15 mi. N.W. of Barrie. For more information contact Nottawasaga Valley Conservation Authority, R.R. #1, Angus, L0M 1B0. 705-424-1479.

Canoeing on Nottawasaga River. Charge, $1.50 per car. $3.50 overnight.

△▲⊙‡♦

2 New Lowell Conservation Area. From Hwy 90, near Angus, travel 8 mi. N.W. along Cty. Rd. 10. Turn W. along Cty. Rd. 9 to New Lowell. For more information contact Notta-

Legend

● No Power Boats
□ Instruction
△ Toilets
✱ Store
⌒ Supervised Swimming

▼ Low Water In Summer
↩ Rental Canoes Available
🏠 Restaurant
▲ Car Camping
⊙ Fireplaces
‡♦ Overnight Canoe Camping

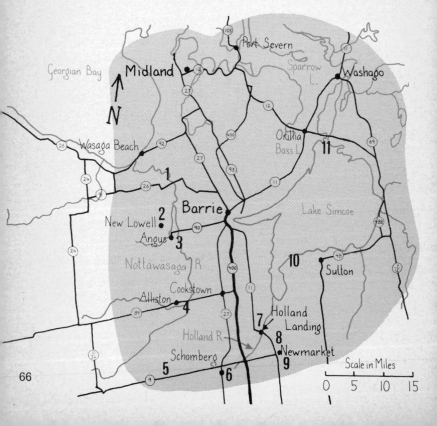

Scale in Miles
0 5 10 15

wasaga Valley Conservation Authority, R.R. #1, Angus, L0M 1B0. 705-424-1479.

Canoeing on a 50 acre reservoir. Rainbow trout are stocked yearly so this reservoir provides excellent opportunities for the fisherman. Charge, $1.50 per car, $3.00 overnight.

●△▲⊙

3 Utopia Conservation Area.
Go 9 mi. W. from Barrie on Hwy 90 to Township Rd. 6 and turn left to area. For more information contact Nottawasaga Region Conservation Authority, R.R. #1, Angus, L0M 1B0. 705-424-1479.

Canoeing on a 20 acre reservoir in 109 acre. Dam has a fish ladder that allows rainbow trout access to the upper reaches of Bear Creek for spawning. Charge, $1.50 per car, $3.00 overnight.

●△▲⊙

4 Nottawasaga River.
Enter from Hwy 89, W. of Cookstown. *Nottawasaga River Canoe Route* brochure available from Nottawasaga Region Conservation Authority, R.R. #1, Angus. L0M 1B0. 705-424-1479.

25 mile river is navigable to Nottawasaga Bay. There are some rapids and/or log jams. Conservation areas available for camping along the way. Day use free. $3.50 overnight at conservation areas.

●△▼⊙♠♠

5 Tottenham Conservation Area.
From Hwy 400, take Hwy 9 W. to Cty. Rd. 10. Turn right and follow to area. For more informa-

tion contact Nottawasaga Region Conservation Authority, R.R. #1, Angus, L0M 1B0. 705-424-1479.

22 acre reservoir in 125 acre conservation area. Charge, $1.50 per car. No overnight camping.

●△⊙

6 Holland Marsh.
Access to S. end of Marsh from Hwy 9, 3 mi. E. of Schomberg.

17 miles of routes available on canals. Day use free. No overnight camping.

7 Holland River.
Start off Hwy 11 at Holland Landing.

An 11 mi. trip is possible by travelling downstream from Holland Landing, then heading upstream on Schomberg R. to Hwy 11, ½ mi. E. of Bradford. Canoeing free. No overnight camping.

8 Roger's Reservoir.
Located about 2½ mi. N. of Newmarket on 2nd Concession. For more information contact South Lake Simcoe Conservation Authority, Box 282, Newmarket, L3Y 4X1. 416-895-1281.

Canoeing on a 40 acre reservoir in an area which serves as natural habitat for a variety of plants and animals that favour marshy regions. Day use free. No overnight camping.

●△

9 Wesley Brooks Memorial Conservation Area.
Located on Water St. in town of Newmarket. For

more information contact South Lake Simcoe Conservation Authority, Box 282, Newmarket, L3Y 4X1. 416-895-1281.

Canoeing on a 13 acre pond. Day use free. No overnight camping.

●△⊙

10 Willow Beach Conservation Area.
Turn off Hwy 48 into Sutton. Head through town to Dalton Rd. and Jackson's Point. Go N. to Lakeshore Dr. and turn W. to area. For more information contact South Lake Simcoe Conservation Authority. Box 282, Newmarket, L3Y 4X1. 416-895-1281.

Canoeing on Lake Simcoe on calm days. Charge, $1.50 per car. No overnight camping.

△⊙

11 Mara Provincial Park.
From Hwy 11, turn E. onto Hwy 12 at Orillia. For more information contact Ministry of Natural Resources, R.R. #2, Maple, L0J 1E0. 416-832-2261.

Canoeing on Lake Simcoe on calm days. Charge, $1.50 per car, $3.50 overnight.

△▲⊙

8 Haliburton Region

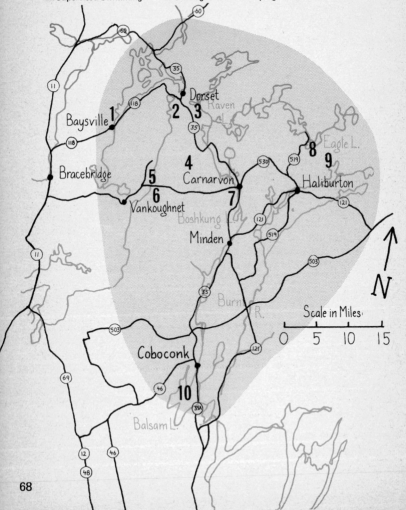

Scale in Miles
0   5   10   15

N

1 South Branch Muskoka River Canoe Route - Baysville to Bracebridge. Baysville access from Hwy 118. *South Branch Muskoka Canoe Route* brochure available from Ministry of Natural Resources, Box 1138, Bracebridge, P0B 1G0. 706-645-5244.

Route is 26 miles long with 11 portages. Before settlement of this area by the white man, this was a main Indian route. Day use free. Campsites along the way.

⚑

2 Wren Lake-Black River-Vankoughnet Route. Start at Wren Lake, S. of Dorset on Hwy 35. Finish at Vankoughnet, 12.5 mi. W. of Carnarvon. *Wilderness Canoe Routes in Haliburton West* brochure available from Ministry of Natural Resources, Minden District, Minden, K0M 2K0. 705-286-1521.

Route is 49 miles long with one portage. On Black Lake, there are long sandy beaches and excellent campsites.

⚑

3 Black Lake Canoe Route. Start at Raven Lake, 4 mi. S. of Dorset on Hwy 35. *Black Lake Canoe Route* brochure available from Ministry of Natural Resources, Box 1138, Bracebridge, P0B 1G0. 705-645-5244.

Route is a 14 mi. circular one with 11 portages. Surveys indicate most of the land was once owned by Chief Yellowhead of Black River. Day use free. Campsites at specific places.

⚑

4 Kandalore Canoe Museum. Located about 8 mi. N. of Carnarvon on Hwy 35. For more information contact Camp Kandalore, Dorset, P0A 1E0. 705-489-2419.

This museum has one of the country's best collections of historical canoes. Free.

△

5 Bentshoe Lake Circle. Bentshoe Lake is 50 yd. N. of Vankoughnet Rd., 12.5 mi. W. of Carnarvon. Trip described in *Wilderness Routes in Haliburton West* brochure.*

7 mi. route passes by ruins of old logging operation. Day use free. Campsites at specific places.

⚑

6 Big East Lake to Vankoughnet. Big East Lake is slightly S. of the Vankoughnet Rd., 12.5 mi. W. of Carnarvon. Trip described in *Wilderness Routes in Haliburton West* brochure.*

12 mi. route with 8 portages. Day use free. Campsites at specific places.

⚑

7 Boshkung-Kennisis-Eagle Lakes Loop. Access to Boshkung Lake from Hwy 35, about 6 mi. N. of Minden. Trip described in *Gull River Routes.* brochure.*

Route is 54 miles long with 18 portages. Day use free. Campsites at specific places.

⚑

8 Eagle Lake to Haliburton Lake. Go N. from town of Haliburton on Hwy 519 to Eagle Lake. Trip described in *Gull River Routes* brochure.*

Good day trip of 10½ miles. Canoeing free. No campsites.

9 Haliburton to Balsam Lake. Take Hwy 121 to Haliburton town dock. Trip described in *Burnt River Routes* brochure.*

Route is 59 miles long. Day use free. Campsites on Crown land.

⚑

10 Balsam Lake to Boshkung Lake. Access to Balsam Lake from Hwy 35A at Coboconk. Trip described in *Gull River Routes* brochure.*

Route is 41 miles N. with 8 portages. The route described in the brochure should be reversed to allow downstream paddling.

Day use free. Campsites at specific places.

⚑

*Brochures describing routes for listings 5 through 10, are available from Ministry of Natural Resources, Minden District, Minden, K0M 2K0. 705-286-1521.

9 Peterborough Region

1 Pigeon River. Access from Omemee on Hwy 7.

River is navigable for about 6½ mi. upstream depending on time of year. Canoeing free. No overnight camping.

▼

2 Emily Provincial Park. Go N. of Hwy 7, slightly E. of Omemee. For more information contact the Ministry of Natural Resources, 322 Kent St. W., Lindsay, K9V 2Z9. 705-324-6121.

Canoeing on Pigeon River and Pigeon Lake. Charge

Legend
● No Power Boats
□ Instruction
△ Toilets
✳ Store
⊟ Supervised Swimming

▼ Low Water In Summer
↝ Rental Canoes Available
🏠 Restaurant
▲ Car Camping
⊙ Fireplaces
⚲ Overnight Canoe Camping

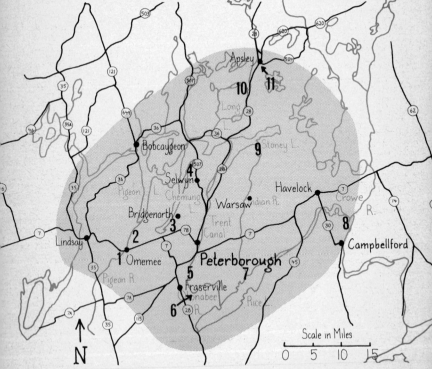

Scale in Miles

0   5   10   15

N

70

$1.50 per car, $3.50 overnight.

△▲◉

3 Chemung Lake Conservation Area. From Hwy 7B, go N. on Cty. Rd. 18 to Bridgenorth. Area is located on S.E. shore of Chemung Lake. For more information contact Otonabee Region Conservation Authority, 727 Lansdowne St. W., Peterborough, K9J 1Z2. 705-745-5791.

Free canoeing on Chemung Lake. No overnight camping.

△◉

4 Selwyn Conservation Area. From Hwy 28, continue on Hwy 507 to Selwyn. Turn W. on 12th Concession of Smith Township for 1 mi. Turn N. to area. For more information contact Otonabee Region Conservation Authority, 727 Lansdowne St. W., Peterborough, K9J 1Z2. 705-745-5791.

Free canoeing on Chemung Lake. No overnight camping.

5 Whitfield Landing. From Hwy 28, take the Fraserville Town Line 2 mi. E. For more information contact Otonabee Region Conservation Authority, 727 Lansdowne St. W., Peterborough, K9J 1Z2, 705-745-5791.

Landing gives access to Otonabee R., part of the Trent Canal System. Canoeing free. No overnight camping.

△◉

6 Squirrel Creek. From Hwy 28, go 2 mi. E. on Wallace Point Rd. For more information contact Otonabee Region Conservation Authority, 727 Lansdowne St. W., Peterborough. K9J 1Z2. 705-745-5791.

Area is on Otonabee R. Charge $1.00 per car, $2.50 overnight.

△▲◉

7 Serpent Mounds Provincial Park. From Hwy 7, go 8 mi. S. on Cty. Rd. 34. For more information contact Ministry of Natural Resources, 322 Kent St. W., Lindsay, K9V 2Z9. 705-324-6121.

Canoeing on Rice Lake. Charge, $1.50 per car, $3.50 overnight.

△▲◉

8 Crowebridge Conservation Area. Go 4½ mi. N. of Campbellford via Northumberland Cty. Rd. 38 to Petherwilk corners, then N. on Seymour Twp. Sideroad 20 for 2 mi. to conservation area. For more information contact Crowebridge Conservation Area, Box 279, Havelock, K0L 1Z0. 613-778-3024.

Canoeing on Crowe R. Charge, $1.00 per car, $2.50 overnight.

△▲◉

9 Indian River. Access from McCracken's Landing on Stoney Lake. Hwy 7 is another good access point. For more information ask for *Indian River Canoe Route* brochure from Otonabee Region Conservation Authority, 727

Lansdowne St. W., Peterborough, K9J 1Z2. 705-745-5791.

26 mile river flows through transition from Canadian Shield to St. Lawrence Lowland. Scenery on route encompasses underground streams, 200 ft. high cliffs, and a restored 19th century sawmill.

▼▲♣

10 Long Lake to Buckhorn Route. Go 35 mi. N. from Peterborough on Hwy 28 to Public Access Point on Long Lake. For more information ask for *Canoe Routes in the Burleigh-Harvey Recreation Zone* from Ministry of Natural Resources, Minden District, Minden, K0M 2K0. 705-286-1521.

Described route is 30 miles long and ends in Stoney Lake.

▼▲♣

11 Eel's Creek Canoe Route. Start at Apsley on Hwy 28. For more information ask for *Eel's Creek Canoe Route* brochure from Ministry of Natural Resources, 322 Kent St. W., Lindsay, K9V 2Z9. 705-324-6121.

Described route is 23.5 mile trip to Stoney Creek with 19 portages. There is camping at specific places.

▲♣

10 Eastern Region

1 Presqu'ile Provincial Park. From Hwy 2, go S. at Brighton. For more information contact Ministry of Natural Resources, 322 Kent St. W., Lindsay, K9V 2Z9. 705-324-6121.

Canoeing on Presqu'ile Bay. Charge, $1.50 per car, $3.50 overnight.
△▲

2 Sandbanks Provincial Park. From Trenton, follow Hwy 33 S. for 15 mi. For more information contact Ministry of Natural Resources, Napanee District, Postal Bag 3040,

Legend
- ● No Power Boats
- ▢ Instruction
- △ Toilets
- ✳ Store
- ⊃ Supervised Swimming

- ▼ Low Water In Summer
- ↩ Rental Canoes Available
- 🏠 Restaurant
- ▲ Car Camping
- ⊙ Fireplaces
- ⚑ Overnight Canoe Camping

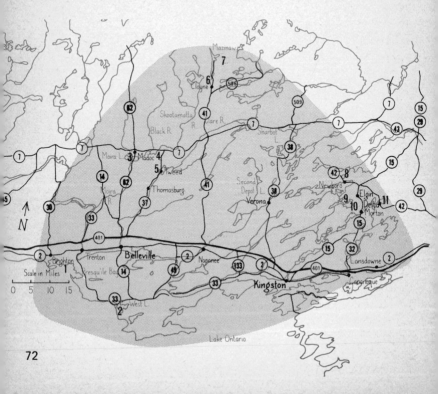

72

Napanee, K0K 2R0. 613-393-3314.

Canoeing on West Lake. Toward the west are beautiful white sand hills. Charge, $1.50 per car, $3.50 overnight.

△✳☉▲◉

3 Moira River to Cannifton.
Access is from the island between the two bridges on Hwy 62 that cross Moira Lake.*

River route from Hwy 62 to Cannifton is 46.5 mi. Some sections get very low in late summer. Good fishing for pickerel, pike, bass. Camp sites along the route. Canoeing free.

▼▲♉

4 Black River.
Access is where Hwy 7 crosses the Black River, E. of Madoc.*

A pleasant 2½ mile upstream paddle with one or two liftovers. Canoeing free. No overnight camping.

▼

5 Clare River.
Start at Memorial Park in Tweed. Trip ends at second bridge up Clare R.*

Clare River received its name when a chain bearer named Clare of the first survey team in the area fell through the ice. Canoeing free. No overnight camping.

6 Skootamatta River-Cloyne to Hwy 7.
At N. end of Cloyne on Hwy 41, take the 1st sideroad W. Turn S. at fork 1 mi. in and follow this road for 2 mi. Put in at the bridge which crosses Skootamatta Lake*.

This is a 31 mile trip involving 27 portages. On route, there is a stone cairn marking the location of an Indian corn grinding hole. Canoeing free.

▲♉

7 Kishkebus Canoe Routes.
Start at Bon Echo Provincial Park. *Kishkebus Canoe Route* brochure is available from Mississippi Valley Conservation Authority, Box 419, Carleton Place, K0A 1J0. 613-257-4272.

Route is 13 miles long with 3 portages. Route passes Indian pictographs. On portage to Shabomeka (Indian word for cranberry) Lake there is an impressive stand of 30-50 ancient sugar maple and yellow birch. Free camping on crown land.

▲♉

8 Newboro Route.
Go to Newboro on Hwy 42 and begin trip from Newboro Locks. Trip described in Canoe Route #1 brochure**.

20 mi. circular route is on the Rideau Canal System. Campsites along the way. Canoeing free.

▲♉

9 Chaffey's Locks Route.
Turn W. on Cty Rd. from Hwy 15 just N. of Elgin. Trip described in Canoe Route #2 brochure**.

Campsites along the way. Canoeing free.

▲♉

10 Jone's Falls Route.
From Hwy 15, turn W. just N. of Morton. Trip described in Canoe Route #3 brochure**.

12 mi. circular route is on the Rideau Canal System. The Giant Horseshoe Dam at John's Falls was built by one man and some horse power in the early 1800s. Canoeing free.

▲♉

11 Delta to Gananoque.
Start at Municipal Park in Delta, located on Hwy 42. Trip described in Canoe Route #4 brochure**.

60 mi. route to Gananoque. The more experienced canoeist may extend this trip to Kingston on the St. Lawrence R. Caution: there are many power boats and there is possible rough water. Canoeing free.

▲♉

*A brochure, "Moira Watershed Canoe Route Guide" describing routes for listings 3 to 6 are available from the Moira River Conservation Authority, Box 68, Cannifton, 705-968-8688.

**Brochures describing routes in listings 8 to 11 are available from Cataraqui Region Conservation Authority, 837 Princess Street, Kingston, K7L 1G8. 613-546-9965.

11 Parry Sound Region

Legend
- ● No Power Boats
- ▢ Instruction
- △ Toilets
- ✳ Store
- ⌣ Supervised Swimming
- ▼ Low Water In Summer
- ⌣ Rental Canoes Available
- 🏠 Restaurant
- ▲ Car Camping
- ☉ Fireplaces
- ▲▲ Overnight Canoe Camping

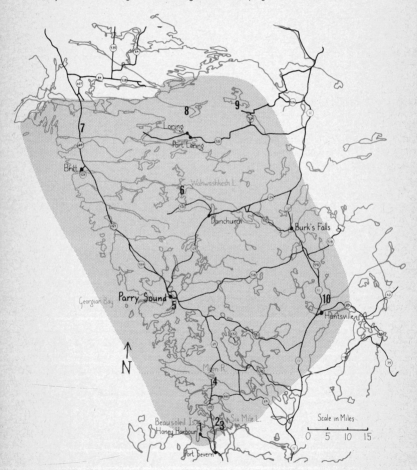

1 Beausoleil Island. At Port Severn, turn W. onto Hwy 501. Go to the government dock in Honey Harbour.

It is possible to paddle the 2.3 mi. to Beausoleil Island in calm weather. This island is part of Georgian Bay Islands National Park.

♠♣

2 Six Mile Lake Provincial Park. Located on Hwy 103, 6 mi. N. of Port Severn. For more information contact Six Mile Provincial Park, c/o Ministry of National Resources, Coldwater, L0K 1E0. 705-686-3342.

Canoeing on Six Mile Lake. Charge $1.50 per car, $3.50 overnight.

△▲⊙♠♣

3 Gibson and McDonald Canoe Routes. Start at Six Mile Lake Provincial Park, 6 mi. N. of Port Severn*.

The McDonald Route is a 24 mi. trip, skirting Georgian Bay and has 5 portages. The Gibson route is 35 mi. with 8 portages. Both routes go through rugged Muskoka landscape. Outside the park, camping is free on crown land.

♠♣

4 Moon River Canoe Route. Take Hwy 103 to Moon River bridge*.

Route is a 24 mi. round trip with 12 portages. The river was used by lumber companies to float logs from Lake Muskoka to Georgian Bay. Gravel road

to the access point is in poor condition. Free camping on crown land.

♠♣

5 Smoked Pickerel Canoe Route. Start at the dock in Parry Sound*.

Route goes through some of the 30,000 islands that dot Georgian Bay.Ojibway Indians used the route as nomad hunters, shifting camp inland to catch and smoke the spawning pickerel. Free camping on crown land.

♠♣

6 Magnetawan Canoe Route. Take Hwy 124 to Dunchurch, then Hwy 520 N. and W. to Wahwashkesh Lake access road. Follow the road to lake*.

Route is a 47 mi. loop with 18 portages. Evidence of the early logging days can still be seen when passing old river drivers. Free camping on crown land.

♠♣

7 Pickerel River Canoe Route. Follow Hwy. 69 to Grundy Park*.

Route is approximately 36 mi. with 8 portages. Voyageurs used the Pickerel and Key waterways for hundreds of years. Outside the park, camping free.

♠♣

8 Wolf and Pickerel Canoe Route. Go W. on Hwy 522 to Loring. Turn N. at Loring on township road to public access point located near bridge*.

Route is 38 mi. with one portage. Interesting stands of solid white pine along the way. Camping free on crown land.

♠♣

9 Dokis Canoe Route. Start at Restoule Provincial Park, accessible from Hwy 534*.

This 55 mi. route circles the Dokis Indian Reserve. Excellent fishing. Camping free outside of park.

♠♣

10 Arrowhead Provincial Park. Located N. of Huntsville on Hwy 11*.

Canoeing available on Arrowhead Lake. Charge $1.50 per car, $3.50 overnight.

△✳▲

*Brochures describing the routes for listings 3 to 10 are available from the Ministry of Natural Resources, 4 Miller Street, Parry Sound, P2A 1S8. 705-746-2141. Ask for brochures by name.

Where to canoe beyond Central Ontario

The 250,000 lakes and waterways in Ontario make the province one of the most attractive places in the world to canoe. For longer trips, you can do no better than to head for the Canadian Shield, which reaches far across northern Ontario. As wilderness canoeing becomes more popular, the north becomes more enticing because of its relative solitude. Many routes through this area are described in the provincial government publication entitled *Northern Ontario Canoe Routes* (you can use the tear-out page at the back of the book to order it).

The fur traders of the 18th century travelled right across Canada to the Rockies in search of new sources of beaver. Because of Canada's natural drainage pattern, the entire area east of the Rockies presents no insurmountable problems for the experienced canoeist. Even today, it is possible to paddle the approximately 2,400 miles from Edmonton to Montreal, with the longest portage being nine miles. If in the pursuit of wilderness canoeing you want to go outside of Ontario, a copy of *Canada Canoe Routes* by Nick Nickels (see books page 78) is a worthwhile investment.

For those of you who want to become a canoe instructor, the Canadian Canoe Association runs a Canoe Instructors' School. Every June, they offer a ten day course. For more information write:

Canoe Instructors' Course, c/o Claude Cousineau, Faculty of Recreation, University of Ottawa, Ottawa, K1N 6N5

For those living in the Ottawa area, canoeing opportunities are numerous. Of course the Rideau River and Rideau Canal that flow right through the nation's capital offer delightful day trips. Maps of adjacent parkland administered by the National Capital Commission are available by contacting the Commission at 48 Rideau St. Ottawa K1N 5W9, 613-992-4231. But for secluded wilderness trips with solitude and indefinite length, Quebec is the answer. The *Guide des Rivieres du Québec*, published in French by the Federation Quebecoise de Canot-Kayak, contains 288 pages of canoe routes in this province. Its cost is $4.50 and is distributed by: Messageries du Jour Inc., 8255 rue Durocher, Montreal H3N 2A8, Quebec.

Trips, clubs, information sources

Books

Here are a few of the many books available on canoeing:

A Guide to Canoe Camping, Luther A. Anderson, Reilly and Lee, Chicago, 1969.

Canada Canoe Routes, Nick Nickels, Trent Publishing Associates, Box #479, Lakefield, Ont. (Many other canoeing books are available, write directly.)

Fur Trade Routes of Canada/Then and Now, Eric Morse, Queen's Printer, Ottawa, 1969.

North American Canoe Country, Calvin Rutstrum, Collier-MacMillan, New York, 1965.

Pole, Paddle and Portage, Complete Guide to Canoeing. Bill Riviere, Van Nostrand, New York, 1969.

Wilderness Canoeing, John W. Malo, MacMillan, New York, 1971.

The Wilderness Route Finder, Calvin Rutstrum, MacMillan, New York, 1967.

Clubs

There are two types of canoe clubs and they differ from each other in their approach to canoeing. The seventeen Ontario clubs of the Canadian Canoe Association focus on flat water racing. Club facilities are usually located on a suitable body of water and some clubs own canoes and kayaks. The nine clubs of the Ontario Wild Water Affiliation meet on various rivers to practise whitewater skills. Most members have their own craft - usually kayaks or whitewater canoes.

Both organizations offer instruction and some give winter indoor pool sessions. Some clubs are greatly involved in competition canoeing and produce our Olympic competitors, while others are more recreational in tone. For information on all the canoeing clubs it is best to contact their coordinating organization - **Canoe Ontario,** c/o Sport Ontario, 559 Jarvis St., Toronto, Ontario, M4Y 2J1. 416-964-8655.

Many nature clubs, conservation organizations, and ski clubs turn to canoeing in the summer and organize outings for their members.

Organized Trips and Instruction

One of the best ways to get started in canoeing and learn wilderness skills is to go on a trip with people who know what they are doing. Most groups offering canoe trips also provide equipment so this is a good way too to check out the sport before you spend money on gear.

Trips and courses vary widely in form and price. Package canoe trips range from $15 to $100 per person per day, with most in the $20 to $30 range. The most expensive will give you a personally guided trip, tailor-made for your small party - everything included. There are many organizations offering a schedule of trips. You travel with other canoeists. In this category, the higher priced outfits ($25-$30 per day) will provide pre-trip briefing and instruction, quality equipment, excellence and variety in food, and several staff with each trip. Generally if you pay more you get more. All the groups listed below are reputable but when comparison shopping you should still ask questions about how many people will be going on the trip, how many leaders will be going along, the qualifications of the leaders, the number of years the organization has been in business, what is and what isn't provided for you, quality of equipment and what sort of meals you can expect. It's also a good idea to talk to one of the leaders to see if your ideas about wilderness camping are compatible.

Organizations

Algonquin Waterways Wilderness Trips, 271 Danforth Ave., Toronto M4K 1N2 416-469-1727.
Beginners weekends to extended whitewater trips with pre-trip training. Instructional weekends as well. (Authors Ian Scott and Mavis Kerr instruct and lead canoe trips with this organization.)
Association of Student Councils, 44 St. George St., Toronto, M5S 2E4. 416-962-8404.
Week long trips in Algonquin for young people 17 to 30.
Black Feather Wilderness Canoe Trips, 415 Tweedsmuir Ave., Ottawa, K1Z 5N6. 613-722-2883.
Trips six days or more, many in Quebec.
Camp Kipawa Wilderness Adventures, 31 Burton Rd., Toronto, M5P 1V1. 416-488-5424.
Trips of one week or more in the far north - in Ontario, Quebec, and Saskatchewan.
Federation of Ontario Naturalists, 1262 Don Mills Rd., Don Mills, M3B 2W7. 416-444-8419.
Nature-oriented canoe trips.
Georgian College Summer School of the Arts, 401 Duckworth St., Barrie, L4M 3X9. 705-728-1951.
Canoeing courses in the Georgian Bay area and canoe trips around Ontario.
Headwaters, P.O. Box #288, Temagami, P0H 2H0. Wilderness programs of two weeks or more - trips and instruction.
Jeff Miller, 310 Garyray Dr., Weston, M9L 1P4. 416-742-5140.
Exclusive expensive guided trips for very small groups.
Madawaska Kanu Camp, 2 Tuna Court, Don Mills, M3A 3L1. 416-447-8845.
Whitewater school for kayaks and covered canoes.
National and Provincial Parks Association of Canada, 47 Colborne St., Suite 308, Toronto, M5E 1E3. 416-366-3494.
Canoe trips in natural areas across Canada including Quetico and several rivers in Ontario.
Ontario Nature Tours, 1164 Broadview Ave., Toronto, M4K 2S5. 416-422-4830.
Canoe camping weeks in Killarney. Nature study out of a base camp.
Seneca College, R.R. #3, King City, L0G 1K0. 416-884-9901.
Wilderness trips and basic canoeing instruction.
Voyageur Schools, King St., Millbrook, L0A 1G0. 705-932-2131.
Whitewater courses, also some trips.

Trips, clubs, information sources

Continued

Wanapitei Wilderness Experiences
(Camp Wanapitei near Temagami),
7 Engleburn Place, Peterborough, K9H
1C4. 705-743-3774. Tripping camp for
young people plus adult trips eight days
or more in northern Ontario and Quebec.
YMCA of Metropolitan Toronto Camping Service, 36 College St., Toronto,
M5G 1K8. 416-920-6010.
Canoe trips for teenagers.

Other Information

For more information on canoeing
classes or trips or clubs in your area
check with your YM-YWCA, the
Parks and Recreation branch of
your municipal government, your
nearby provincial Ministry of Natural Resources office, your local
conservation authority, and the
nearest office of the provincial
government's Sports and Recreation Bureau (Ministry of Community and Social Services). Associated
with the Sports and Recreation
Bureau is an organization called
Canoe Ontario, c/o Sport Ontario,
559 Jarvis St., Toronto, M4Y 2J1,
416-964-8655. This is a blanket
organization working to coordinate
all canoeing organizations in the
province - canoe touring as well as
flat water and whitewater racing.
They may be able to answer your
questions.

Some community colleges and universities also offer courses and canoeing outings. Check high school
evening classes as well.

Canoeing for Young People

Many of the canoe tripping groups
listed in this book welcome children either with their parents or on
their own. However, the most common way for youngsters to begin
canoeing is at summer camp. The
Ontario Camping Association,
Suite #203, 102 Eglinton Ave. E.,
Toronto, M4P 1E1. 416-486-8630,
will send you a directory listing
member camps and describing the
activities offered by each. And
TORONTO LIFE magazine, February 1975, did an excellent critical
survey of camps. Many young
people also have been introduced to
canoeing through the Boy Scouts
or Girl Guides and recently some
schools have started outing clubs
with canoe tripping programs for
their students. Some camps and
groups unfortunately have been
known to send out trips with young
inexperienced leaders incapable of
handling the kind of emergencies
that can arise in the wilderness - so
you should check out canoeing
programs very carefully.